Christoph Bäumel
David Gerstner

R&D Resources in
Multibusiness Firms

D1800093

Christoph Bäumel
David Gerstner

R&D Resources in Multibusiness Firms

Measuring Relatedness

VDM Verlag Dr. Müller

Copyright © 2007 VDM Verlag Dr. Müller e. K. and licensors
All rights reserved. Saarbrücken 2007
Contact: info@vdm-verlag.de
Cover image: www.purestockx.com
Publisher: VDM Verlag Dr. Müller e. K., Dudweiler Landstr. 125 a, 66123 Saarbrücken, Germany
Produced by: Lightning Source Inc., La Vergne, Tennessee/USA
           Lightning Source UK Ltd., Milton Keynes, UK

Copyright © 2007 VDM Verlag Dr. Müller e. K. und Lizenzgeber
Alle Rechte vorbehalten. Saarbrücken 2007
Kontakt: info@vdm-verlag.de
Coverbild: www.purestockx.com
Verlag: VDM Verlag Dr. Müller e. K., Dudweiler Landstr. 125 a, 66123 Saarbrücken, Deutschland
Herstellung: Lightning Source Inc., La Vergne, Tennessee/USA
           Lightning Source UK Ltd., Milton Keynes, UK

ISBN: 978-3-8364-1400-5

ABSTRACT

Almost half a century of diversification research supports the suggestion that related resources lead to a superior performance of multi-business firms (Tanriverdi and Venkatraman, 2005, p.97). Nonetheless, no direct measurement concept on a complete resource base of a single business function exists up to now. This book focuses on that gap. It is based on the understanding of R&D and its resources. The focus on R&D was taken as it is a functional area where resources are very often misunderstood (Pike et al., 2005, p.111). This understanding is used to develop a questionnaire in order to measure the relatedness of the identified resource base. Besides the core question of relatedness, there are two main hypotheses developed which are also proved later on: (1) Is relatedness similar to the potential synergies of a resource which is tested to be significantly true while (2) knowledge based resources are not tested to be more important for the success of R&D than other resources are. The results suggest that three resources are more related than other resources are. In order of appearance there are the general resources (mobile and immobile ones but all tangible), the internal knowledge which is R&D specific and last but not least the operational structure of R&D (different process structures). These resources are analysed and categorised through splitting them up on a more detailed sub-level with the intention to create a relatedness measure which is able to identify, on the one hand, the related resources between the three resources, but also to highlight the degree of relatedness within these three resources. The measure is able to offer one overall relatedness value that shows to what degree the R&D departments within a multi-business firm are related. Hence this book offers some interesting implications for oncoming studies on measuring relatedness, as it does for practitioners who want to measure the relatedness of R&D.

TABLE OF CONTENT

LIST OF FIGURES

LIST OF TABLES

LIST OF ABBREVIATIONS

BU	business unit
cf	confer
DIT	Department of Trade
e.g.	For example [exempli gratia]
HGB	Handelsgesetzbuch
i.e.	That is [id est]
IT	information technology
MBF	multi-business firm
MBV	market-based view
N/A	not applicable
OECD	Organisation for Economic Co-operation and Development
SIC	Standard Industrial Classification
R&D	research and development
RBV	resource-based view

1 INTRODUCTION PART A

1.1 PROBLEM STATEMENT

Discussing the diversification strategy of a firm automatically leads to the point where the question on possible synergies arises. Especially as one of the key propositions of strategic management literature is that synergies lead to a value of the firm that exceeds the value of its single BUs.[1] This question shows on the one hand that synergies or economies of scope and scale occurring from relatedness are subject to an ongoing discussion in strategic management. On the other hand there is a large practical interest in identifying relatedness within BUs in order to realise additional gains by reducing costs through related resources. Especially as there are tendencies that firms are moving towards medium diversified MBFs.[2] Hence this research area is a central part of the strategic management research.

Four decades of relatedness research found support for the idea that related resources within diversified firms lead to a superior performance.[3] So undergoing research on relatedness seems to be advantageous to analyse diversification and identify possible synergies in order to improve firm performance. In consequence analysing tools based on the resources of firms gained practical importance. The first tools were insufficient because of their distance to the relevant tangible and intangible resources. Another important characteristic was the focus on the relatedness of BUs so that the results of these traditional measures (e.g. continuous or categorical measures) were not as reliable as they were expected to be at first sight.[4] Hence scholars developed patent count based measures and other instruments for an external assessment but still similar problems arose. The most recent approach in diversification assessment was that scholars identified one resource and tried to measure the relatedness of this resource by direct measurement.[5]

---

[1] See Hungenberg (2001), pp.394-411.
[2] See Szeless (2001), p. 126.
[3] See Tanriverdi/Venkatraman (2005), p.97.
[4] See Robins/Wiersema (1995), p.281.
[5] See Tanriverdi (2006).

This book wants to address exactly the problems pointed out before, in order to measure relatedness with a more detailed and precise approach. Another problem occurring in the discussion of relatedness is the lack of literature on direct measures of relatedness. There are only a few publications on this area.[6] Developing such a direct measure of relatedness opens the next problematic area. Especially as literature discusses the underlying resource base only sparsely. This need for information is especially problematic as the resource base of a whole single BU defers from the resource base of a functional area with more specific resources. Hence it is necessary to choose a functional area within a diversified firm which can be analysed with reference to its resources. In this context Research and Development was identified as one of the most important drivers for economic growth on the one hand[7] and as one of the most misunderstood functions within a firm on the other hand. The second statement is supported by PIKE et al. who stated that

"...R&D organizations often do not understand how resources rely on each other to create value which leads to an R&D process that is often stochastic and discontinuous."[8]

This lack of know-how about R&D and its resources points out the necessity to develop a measure that offers a detailed overview on the resources in order to determine the relatedness of these resources to close the gap of current diversification research and functional corporate strategy described before.

1.2 SCOPE AND KEY OBJECTIVES OF THE STUDY

The main objective of this book is to construct a new measurement concept for the relatedness of companies within diversified firms in R&D. This process follows the relevant theoretical approaches of diversification and measuring relatedness. The theoretical fundament for this book is the RBV which represents the state of the art in diversification research. At this point it is important to note that this book

---

[6] See e.g. Tanriverdi/Venkatraman (2005), Tanriverdi (2005), and Tanriverdi (2006).
[7] See Solow (1957), p. 312.
[8] See Pike et al. (2005), p.111.

consists of two parts. Part A covers chapter one to chapter five while Part B comprises chapter six to chapter nine.

The starting point is chapter two, which presents an overview on the theory of diversification. This section defines diversification for this book and elaborates why the RBV is advantageous for a measurement concept. The MBV is also discussed but with less intensity because this approach is not applied. Another important part of this chapter is the outline of different motives for diversification. The general objectives for diversification, here especially (dis-)synergies, are necessary in order to understand the complexity of the resource base which is part of chapter three. Beforehand it is crucial to point out the relevance of R&D which is a complex and often misunderstood function for the firm.

The main objective of the third chapter is to offer a detailed answer on the question: "What is R&D in detail?" Hence R&D is classified and an overview on possible organisational approaches of R&D is given. This information is necessary in order to understand the relevant resources for the function of R&D which is analysed in chapter four.

As outlined before chapter four uses the information of chapter three for identifying the complete resource base of R&D within a firm. Besides this classification of resources there is a detailed identification of potential synergies of the resources in R&D based on the theoretical explanations in chapter two. These potential synergies are discussed, as this is one of the central questions for diversification researchers: "Can relatedness also be described as potential synergies?" The empirical part of this book tries to answer this question by using primary data.

Before measuring relatedness empirically it is relevant to get an overview on the development of relatedness measures in diversification research. Hence the fifth chapter deals with existing measures of relatedness. Focusing on indirect measures to understand why these measures are not easy to realise and are in consequence not in the centre of this book. But in order to point out some possible approximations for an indirect measure and to structure weaknesses that might be avoided for the measure developed in this book this information are necessary.

Nonetheless the main objective is to gain deeper knowledge about relatedness assessment in order to optimise the measures of this book.

Part B begins by implementing the information delivered by the first five chapters into a questionnaire. This questionnaire is mainly focusing on measuring the relatedness of the resource base of R&D. Beside this main objective there are three hypotheses formulated. While the first is asking whether relatedness and potential synergies are identical, the second and the third ones are asking for the impact of the single resource to the success of R&D in different detail. The analysis of these hypotheses and the whole questionnaire are part of chapter seven.

Chapter seven is – as outlined – focusing on the descriptive analysis of the data delivered by the performed survey. This analysis is divided into a univariate and a multivariate analysis. In the beginning an overview on the data available is given. In a second step the univariate analysis is especially answering the question of resource relatedness while the multivariate analysis is trying to answer the hypotheses. The knowledge created through this analysis is used for the development of a measurement concept in chapter eight.

In chapter eight the centre of attention is set on the measurement concept. Beside the direct measurement of related resources in chapter seven another important objective of this book is to construct a measure for relatedness of R&D. The concept should be easy to understand and to use in practice. Hence the identification of the relevant measures and their operationalisation are in the centre of this chapter.

Finally, the last chapter will provide an overview on the information produced before, in order to give some concluding remarks for future research on measuring relatedness in general and on measuring relatedness in R&D. The whole process of this book is graphically displayed in Figure 1-1.

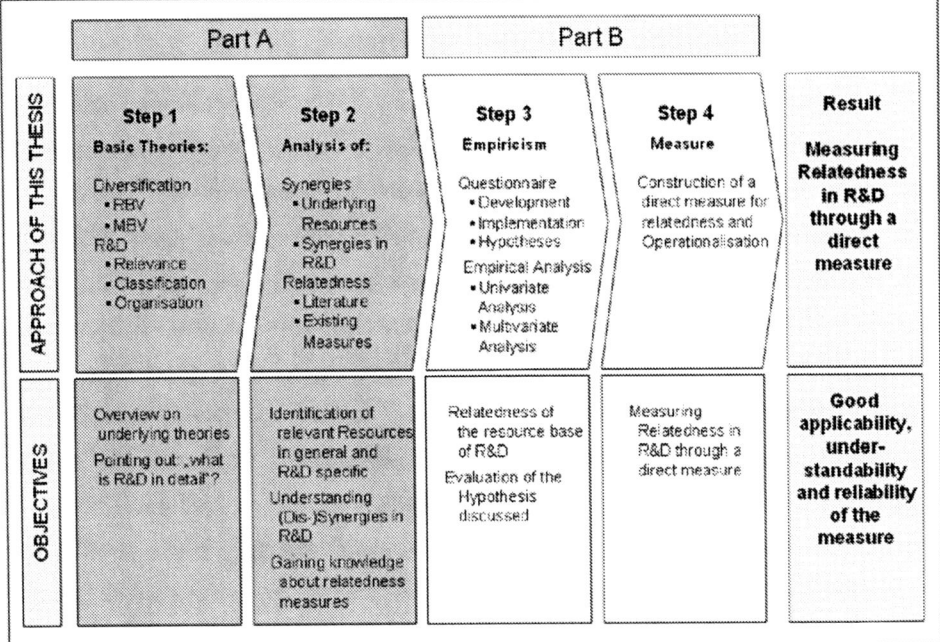

Figure 1-1 Overview on the approach and objectives of this book

Source: Own development

2 BASIC THEORIES ON DIVERSIFICATION

Diversification research was initiated in the early 1950s and developed along to a very well recognised area in managerial research.[9] During the first two decades scholars tried to develop a theoretical framework for diversification.[10] The interest in diversification was stimulated by the era of "conglomerates" from 1955 until 1968. During this period various companies differentiated into industries which could not be counted as their core competence industry. In the early 1970s a crisis followed when the conglomerates noticed that management of such a large and fast expanding company bears many risks.[11] Hence scholars focused their attention on empirical studies to address these arising problems. The crucial question for scientists is to measure diversification and to find out whether it influences the success of a firm in a positive or negative way.[12] The answer to this question is important to explain the existence of MBFs[13]. However studies pointed out that diversified firms destroy value which opposed the arguments of many other researchers.[14] WILLIAMSON explained the existence of MBFs with the higher efficiency which is due to the transaction cost advantages.[15] This seems to be the only possible explanation for the existence and the motives to form a diversified firm. Hence the most important research streams and fundamental theories are discussed in this chapter. Especially the definition and the classification of diversification are introduced first. Afterwards the perspective for the book is introduced by discussing strengths and weaknesses of the MBV and especially the RBV. Finally the motives for diversification are analysed. This gives a first impression on the importance of relatedness within diversified firms.

---

[9] See Fey (1999), p. 7.
[10] See Andrews (1951) pp. 91-107; Ansoff (1957); Penrose (1995); Gort (1962); Ansoff (1965) pp. 127-138; Rumelt (1982), p. 363.
[11] See Lehmann (1993), p.3.
[12] See Montgomery (1994), pp. 163; Palich et al. (2000), p. 155.
[13] Note: Almost all multibusiness firms are at the same time multinationals. Hence this book will use multinational and multibusiness synonymously.
[14] See Gerke/Bank (2003), p.53.
[15] See Williamson (1975) quoted in Hungenberg (2001), p.333

2.1 DEFINITION AND CLASSIFICATION OF DIVERSIFICATION

The definition of diversification in practice and in theory offers a wide scope which leaves space for interpretation.[16] This is the result of numerous different origins of researchers dealing with diversification. Analysing the relevant literature leads to the identification of six schools of thought. These are "Capital Market", "Principle Agent", "Industrial Organization", Organizational Behaviour", "Human Resources" and "Strategic Management".[17] But there were also scholars from other disciplines like business historians, lawyers and others.[18] Thus it is necessary to define the expression used by this book. Diversification derives etymologically from the Latin words "diversus" and "facere". In Italy the word "diversificare" is still existent. The meaning is best reflected by "variety" or "plurality".[19] This etymological definition still leaves room for interpretation which leads to the theoretical development of the different classifications of diversification.

One of the first definitions goes back on ANDREWS who stated that a firm is diversified if it produces or sells more than one product.[20] GORT instead defined diversification as the heterogeneity of markets and resources.

"Two products may be specified as diverse if they belong to separate markets and their cross-elasticities of demand are low and in the short run, the necessary resources employed in the production and distribution of one cannot be shifted to the other."[21]

Another approach was made by RUMELT who defined diversification from the perspective of the served market, which means that "produced and sold products and product lines have no market interaction with each of the firm's other products."[22] The integration of the market and the product perspective was a bridging of diversification and strategy. In this context ANSOFF introduced the "Product-mission matrix" also known as the product-market matrix. Hence diversification is on hand if a company starts a new activity with a new product

---

[16] See Lehmann (1993), p. 18; Reed/Luffman (1986), p. 29.
[17] See Schmidt et al. (2005), p.297.
[18] See Lehmann (1993), pp.6-7.
[19] See Löbler (1988), p. 7.
[20] See Andrews (1951), p. 91.
[21] Gort (1962), p. 8.
[22] Rumelt (1982), p. 363.

which contains new features.[23] This interpretation was subject to further developments by PENROSE and later ABELL, who expanded the product-market concept, which led to four different types of diversification.[24]

The seminal work of ANSOFF had sustainable influence on diversification literature.[25] One important difference is the distinction between "related" and "unrelated" technologies of new products.[26] The various possibilities of diversification are pictured in Figure 2-1.

	Customers	New products	
		Related technology	Related technology
New missions	Same type	Horizontal diversification	
	Firm its own customer	Vertical integration	
	Similar type	(1)* Concentric diversification	(2)*
	New type	(3)*	Conglomerate diversification

Note: (1).Marketing and technology related; (2).Marketing related; (3).Technology related

Figure 2-1 Growth vectors in diversification
Source: Ansoff (1965), p.116.

The relatedness discussed by ANSOFF in the "Diversification Matrix" is based on the MBV and is in consequence not relevant. Especially as the focus of this book lies on the relatedness of resources and on the later introduced RBV which will be discussed in detail in chapter 2.3.4.

---

[23] See Ansoff (1965), p.128.
[24] See Penrose (1995), pp.108-111; Abell (1980), p.169.
[25] See Fey (1999), p.10.
[26] See Ansoff (1965), p.132.

CHANDLER introduced another well-known approach in 1962 that analysed growth and organisational structures of large American firms. He had a similar idea of diversification like ANSOFF and therefore saw diversification as one possible strategy for growth.[27] Other researchers emphasised the importance of administration. Therefore they focused on the influence of diversification on a firm's "administrative structure, systems and other management processes."[28] Summing up two main streams can be highlighted. On the one hand scholars like PENROSE, GORT and RUMELT defined diversification within the dimension of product, market and resources.[29] While on the other hand ANSOFF and RAMANUJAM and VARANDARAJAN only included the products and markets into their definitions.[30] At this point it is important to note that these classifications are process oriented which means that diversification is seen as a dynamic process.[31] As this book is going to develop a scheme to measure the relatedness of R&D it is important to define diversification in contrast to the above definitions within a static context. Hence it is also not necessary to introduce the different possibilities to realise a diversification in more detail as it is a dynamic process. The most important information in this context is that firms are able to diversify on the one hand internally through organic development, licensing and acquisition (products, technologies, etc.) and on the other hand externally through acquisition (firms) and cooperation.[32]

Summarising all the definitions, scholars agree on diversification as the entrance or expansion into a new field of activity which is different from existing activities.[33] This definition is obviously from a dynamic point of view but nonetheless it is a good starting point for the definition of static diversification. Hence a firm is diversified if it consists of fields of activity which are different from each other, which is the so called multi business firm. Two problems occur while analysing this definition. On the one hand the problem of "what is difference" and on the other hand the question which criteria determines the activities of a firm. The problem

---

[27] See Szeless (2001), p.20.
[28] See Ramanujam/Varadarajan (1989), p.525.
[29] See Penrose (1995), p.110; Gort (1962), p.8; Rumelt (1974), p.10.
[30] See Ansoff (1957), p.114; Ramanujam/Varadarajan (1989), p.525.
[31] See Ganz (1991), pp.8.
[32] See Döhmen (1991), pp.223-250.
[33] Cf e.g. Ansoff (1957), p.113; Gort (1962), p.8; Penrose (1963), pp.109 and others.

with "difference" can hardly be solved as there are so many definitions circulating.[34] In contrast to this problem it is clear that the field of activity is determined by the resources a firm uses. Thus it seems obvious that the RBV – discussed later in chapter 2.3.4 – is advantageous for a relatedness measure. Another important question especially with the focus on relatedness research is the relationship between diversification and performance. The literature is still unsettled in this area. These circumstances lead to the introduction of relatedness into the diversification theory on both, the product and the resource side.[35] Hence the following chapter will point out in detail why the resource based view is advantageous compared to the MBV, especially considering the development of a model which can measure relatedness of R&D.

2.2 THE MARKET-BASED VIEW

The MBV was predominant for decades. This sector of economic research was called "industrial organisation" and primarily embossed by MASON and BAIN in the late 1930's and early 1940's.[36] MASON introduced the hypothesis that different behaviour especially in price policies can be explained by different structures of a firms market.[37] This fostered further discussion which led to the idea that market structure can not be seen as autonomous as it is determined by the market behaviour and other influencing factors.[38] This critique was the starting point for a further development. The so called "Structure-Conduct-Performance - Paradigm" or "Industrial Organisation Paradigm" evolved. According to this paradigm market structure is not the only influencing variable but the dominating one. In the 1960's a new discipline called Strategic Planning was introduced.[39] PORTER released as a strategic management researcher a fundamental work on the "Five Competitive Forces" which determine the attractiveness of an industry from the point of view of a sustainable acting and planning company.[40] The five forces take effect on all companies. The five competitive forces are: "the entry of new competitors, the threat of substitutes, the bargaining power of buyers, the

---

[34] See Lehmann (1993), p.23.
[35] See Markides/Williamson (1996), p.341.
[36] See Fey (2001), p.16.
[37] See Mason (1939), p. 73.
[38] See Minderlein (1993), pp.167-168.
[39] See Fey (2001), p.17.
[40] See Hungenberg (2001), pp.84-86.

bargaining power of suppliers, and the rivalry among the existing competitors".[41] The empirical studies performed in this research area predominantly reasoned that the strategy has to be adapted to the existing industry structures. This opposes the MBV resulting in a consequent change in perspective of scholars all over the world.[42] Another dilemma was the selection of the market and the problematic classification of the exact market.[43] Discussing the weaknesses of the MBV, it is important to note that this perspective and the resource based view reflect two sides of the same coin from the point of view of a firm.[44] Therefore both perspectives are important for the management of a diversified firm[45], but focusing only at the products or market side to identify the relatedness of a diversified firm would reach too short.[46] Therefore the following paragraph will primarily give a detailed overview on the RBV and the implications for this book.

2.3 THE RESOURCE-BASED VIEW

The RBV has its roots in PENROSE's publication in the late 1950s.[47] This view of the firm as a bundle of resources was explained as:

"[A] firm is more than an administrative unit; it is also a collection of productive resources the disposal of which between different uses and over time is determined by administrative decision."[48]

This perspective became more important in the 1980s and was completely introduced and accepted at the beginning of the 1990s.[49] Within the next decade it developed to the dominant approach in strategy research.[50] Reasons for this development are on the one hand the weaknesses of the MBV as explained in Chapter 2.2, but on the other hand there was a growing understanding for the

---

[41] See Porter (1998), p.2.
[42] See Fey (2001), p.19 and pp.148-154.
[43] See Anwander (2000), p.38.
[44] See Wernerfelt (1984), p.171.
[45] See Szeless (2001), p.9.
[46] See Stimpert/Duhaime (1997), p.113, more detailed information can be found in Chapter 2.3.3.
[47] See Hoskisson et al. (1999), p.417.
[48] Penrose (1995), p.24.
[49] See Hoskisson et al. (1999), p.417.
[50] See Foss (1998), p.134.

importance of resources in achieving competitive advantages.[51] Also the empirical evidence delivered by a study of ROBINS and WIERSEMA supported the RBV. This study pointed out that the relatedness of resources is more significantly correlated to success than the relatedness of products.[52] In consequence the importance of the resource based view grew. After discussing some reasons for the fast increasing importance of the RBV it is necessary to address the problems of this perspective. One key problem of this approach is the provision of information to perform econometric analysis, especially in the case of intangible resources. This is a key critique on the RBV which was expressed by PORTER or HENDERSON and COCKBURN. [53] Another point of concern is stated by FOSS in 1998. He identified the fundamental problem of the RBV when applying a dynamic perspective.[54] In other words the RBV is a static approach which can only draw a static picture of the moment and is no process oriented approach. Nevertheless the RBV is the status quo in diversification research and is in consequence in the centre of the further developments.[55] To understand the strengths and weaknesses it is important to give a detailed definition of resources and furthermore give an overview on the possible characteristics of resources and potential problems for this book based on these features.

2.3.1 DEFINING RESOURCES

The expression "resource" or asset is not defined uniformly.[56] Some researchers separate capabilities from resources. The literature separates capabilities as competences or know-how which is used to expand the resources.[57] Other scholars define resources as necessary element for capabilities.[58] Some do not postulate this differentiation at all.[59] The discussion on the resource base is deepened in chapter 4.1 with respect to the specific characteristics of R&D. This brief overview is focusing on a broad classification of a firm's general resource base.

---

[51] See Barney (1991), p.99, Peteraf (1993), p.179.
[52] See Robins/Wiersema (1995).
[53] See Lieberman/Montgomery (1998), p.1112.
[54] See Foss (1998), p.144.
[55] See e.g. Farjoun (1994), pp.186-188.
[56] See Szeless (2001), p.10.
[57] See Markides/Williamson (1996).
[58] See Grant (1991), p.119.
[59] See Barney (1991), pp.99ff; Peteraf (1993), p.180.

In this book resources in a wider sense are defined as capabilities on the one hand and resources on the other hand. Considering the interrelation of resources according to this definition and capabilities and the linked problem to separate these two neat from each another[60] leads to the conclusion that this level will not be part of further discussions. Hence only resources in a narrower interpretation will be observed in this book. This narrow interpretation leads to the distinction of material or tangible resources and immaterial or intangible resources which is the relevant definition for this book.[61] CHANDLER described the importance of tangible and intangible resources as follows:

"Of these resources, trained personnel with manufacturing, marketing and engineering, scientific and managerial skills often become even more valuable than warehouses, plants, offices and other physical factors."[62]

This statement on the importance of resources and here especially the intangibles explain very well why this book attaches importance to the tangible but especially to the intangible resources. Especially as one specific characteristic of R&D is the predominance of intangible assets. This aspect will be allowed by a more detailed splitting into two concepts which will be pictured in Figure 2-2. The single resources are based on (a) Organisational Resources (e.g. Brand, Image, communication culture, culture in general) and (b) Knowledge (e.g. individual know-how, patents, and production technologies).[63]

---

[60] See Canals (2000), p.118.
[61] See Wernerfelt (1984), p.172.
[62] Chandler (1962), p.383.
[63] Several authors (e.g. Wernerfelt (1984), p.172; Fey (1999), p.20; Szeless (2001), p.10-12.) enumerate some resources like technological or human resources, but there was no structured picture available on this level. A more detailed introduction with explanations to the development and meaning of the relevant resources will be made in Chapter 4.

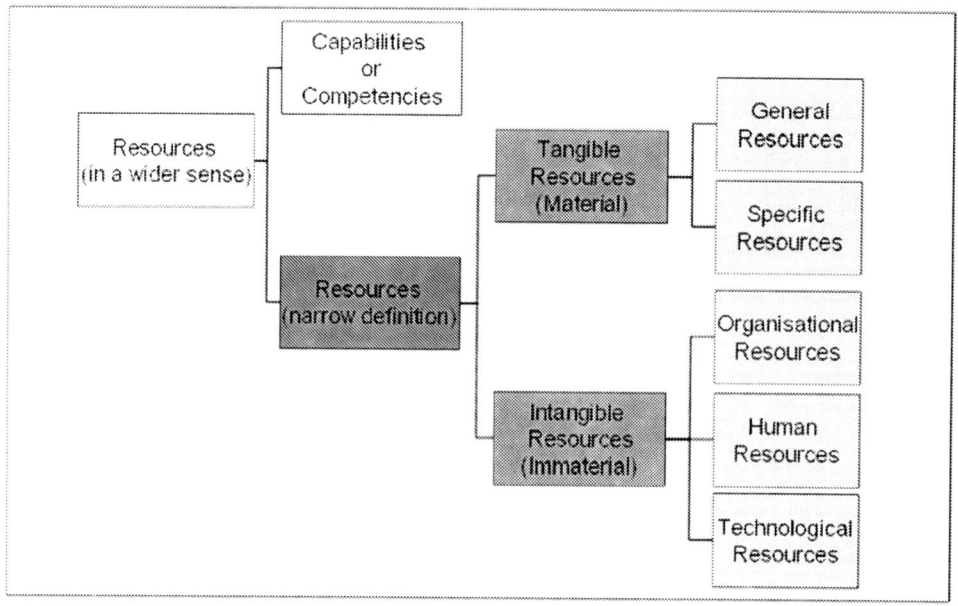

Figure 2-2 Structured overview on resource definitions

Source: own development following a basic structure of Wernerfelt (1984), p.172.

The reason for this far reaching extension of the definition is that this structure is a fundamental precondition to identify possible connections between different R&D departments and in consequence an important step to detect possible synergies in R&D due to relatedness. Financial resources are other important assets which will be factored out of further discussions even if scholars regularly identify them as a separate resource in addition to the tangible and intangible resources.[64] One reason for this decision is the complexity of this financial dimension. Further reasons are explained in chapter 4.2.2.

2.3.2 ATTRIBUTES OF RESOURCES

One of the main concerns of the RBV is to outline the necessary terms for sustainable competitive advantages[65] based on the resources of a firm.[66] In this context it is important to note that the discussion of sustainable competitive advantages and first-mover advantages is not part of this book. This is based on

---

[64] See e.g. Chatterjee/Wernerfelt (1991), pp.34-35.
[65] More information on the definition of „competitive advantage" and „sustained competitive advantages" can be found in Barney (2001), p.102-103.
[66] See Fey (2001), p.20.

the decision to exclude capabilities from the resource definition in chapter 2.3.1. For this reason this book is strongly focused to give a detailed view on possible relations of resources in R&D departments.

Literature states six relevant attributes of resources. One fundamental attribute is the so-called resource heterogeneity of a firm; another important characteristic is the immobility of a resource.[67] Resource heterogeneity is reflected through the asymmetric equipment in resources of a firm, which again corresponds with the fact the factor markets are incomplete.[68] Thus resources have certain degrees of immobility. Another attribute is the relevance of a resource which means that it is important to create or implement a strategy which improves efficiency and effectiveness.[69] Rareness of a resource is also a characteristic, which is existent if a resource is only available to a certain extent which does not allow complete competition.[70] The last important attribute is of minor importance for this book as it is based on the capabilities. Hence capabilities have to be unique in their composition, have to have value adding function, have to be inimitable[71] and finally cannot be substituted.[72] The impact of these characteristics on the motives for diversification will be discussed in chapter 2.4.1.2. After introducing briefly the relevant resource in a very general manner the following chapter gives a first overview on the possible relatedness of the described resources.

2.3.3 RELATEDNESS OF RESOURCES

Relatedness is a very central expression in this book. The scope of relatedness is best covered by one definition for this book, but there are several definitions which are certainly important to note before.[73] Especially the classical relatedness which is the similarity or complementarity of product attributes. In this case the criteria for relatedness are defined by the Standard Industrial Classification[74].[75] Problematic

---

[67] See Barney (1991), p.103.
[68] See Dierickx/Cool (1989), pp.1505-1506.
[69] See Barney (1991), p.102.
[70] See Szeless (2001), p.16.
[71] Further information on the imitation of resources are discussed in Szeless (2001), pp.17-19.
[72] See Barney (1991), p.105-106.
[73] See Farjoun (1998), p.612.
[74] More information on the SIC-Codes (especially limitations) can be found in Villalonga (2004), pp.479-482 and Robins/Wiersema (1995), pp.281-282.
[75] See Gort (1962), pp.57-58.

with this definition of relatedness from a theoretical point of view is that there are several dimensions necessary to analyse relatedness correctly like STIMPERT and DUHAIME discovered.[76] Further problems of the relatedness of products are the constrained range of diversification possibilities due to the search which is focused on applications for physical artefacts. It is also important to note that these resources are more specific (especially product specific) and in consequence lead to a limited range of industries where they can be applied.[77] This knowledge is recognised by later studies and leads to the focus on skill based resources or better intangible resources of a firm.[78] A modern definition of resource relatedness is stated by FARJOUN:

"..., the new concept of relatedness views each industry or line of business as a combination of occupational skills or bodies of knowledge required to produce a product."[79]

This book will not focus on the relatedness of industries mentioned in the definition which was intensely analysed by ROBINS and WIERSEMA and other scholars.[80] The key attention will be on the relatedness of BUs due to related resources and here specifically the relatedness of R&D resources. The last section will discuss the relevant perspective within the RBV for this book.

2.3.4 STRUCTURE BASED SCHOOL OF THOUGHT

Two different schools of thought are discussed in literature. The first to be mentioned is the "traditional focus" or the "process school" which is highlighting the dynamic aspects of a resource to sustain competitive advantage in a changing market environment.[81] Hence the development of the resources is in the centre of observation, but still it is important to note that not all dynamic perspectives are evolutionary.[82] The second school of thought is the relevant one for this book as it is the structure-based school of thought which is basically describing and defining

---

[76] See Stimpert/Duhaime (1997), p.122.
[77] See Farjoun (1998), p.613.
[78] See Farjoun (1998), p.612.
[79] See Farjoun (1998), p.612.
[80] See Robins/Wiersema (1995), p.293; see also Scherer (1982) and Farjoun (1994).
[81] See Schulze (1994), p.142, but also Foss (1997), p.138.
[82] See Foss (1997), p.138.

the characteristics of resources which are necessary to achieve competitive advantages.[83] This perspective will be predominant for obvious reasons in chapter four when possible relations and in consequence synergies in R&D are described but beforehand it is necessary to examine the reasons for diversification.

2.4 MOTIVES FOR DIVERSIFICATION

Focusing on the objective of this book which is to develop an assessment of relatedness of R&D, it seems to be fundamentally necessary to point out the positive and negative effects caused by diversification activities. As empirical tests performed in the past did not give a clear answer on the question whether diversification correlates with success and therefore whether positive effects or whether negative effects prevail.[84] A similar discussion exists about the question whether a diversified firm with related resources performs better than a firm which is unrelated within the underlying resources of its BUs.[85] The problems of the empirical tests are not in the centre of discussion but are nevertheless important to note. Hence the following paragraph will give an overview on the different motives of diversification developed in different areas of research. The main focus will be on synergies as this is the most important phenomena in the context of this book.

2.4.1 SYNERGIES

2.4.1.1 DEFINITION AND DEVELOPMENT OF THE SYNERGY CONCEPT

In the past ANSOFF introduced the discussion about the advantages of diversification with his symbolic equation "2+2=5".[86] Scholars describe synergies in this context as

„the ability of two or more units or companies to generate greater value working together than they could working apart".[87]

---

[83] See Barney (1991), pp.101-112.
[84] See Fey (2001), pp.117-120.
[85] See Chatterjee/Wernerfelt (1991), p.33.
[86] See Ansoff (1965), p.79.
[87] Goold/Campbell (1998), p.133.

Some even state that synergies are the only reason to diversify a firm or at least the most important one.[88] This is mainly the result of a wide definition. "Synergy" derives from the Greek and consists of "syn" which means to combine or to unite while "ergon" means to work or to be active. Therefore synergies means that single parts work together united as a whole. This definition might not be detailed enough for this book. ANSOFF identified four areas within a company where synergies might arise, "sales synergy", "operating synergy", "investment synergy" and "management synergy".[89] Hence the focus was on material synergies. PORTER saw the potential synergies similarly to ANSOFF. He stated in a well known article that the material synergies are of higher value for a diversified firm.[90] This focus on tangible synergies changed in the following years when the focus of researchers shifted to the intangible synergies.[91] It is important to note that material synergies primarily lead to economies of scope and scale as some activities of different BUs can be collectively accomplished.[92] Immaterial synergies primarily realise learning curve effects and economies of scope.[93] Another classification is mentioned by NAYYAR. He distinguished tangible synergies where "markets", "distribution systems", "product and process technologies" or "manufacturing facilities" correspond from intangible synergies where "technologies" and other "routines" and "repertoires" correspond.[94] Henceforth scholars focused their attention on intangible synergies. PRAHALAD and BETTIS introduced "the concept of dominant general management logic" and the idea that managers play an important role in a diversified firm.[95] A further theory was the one of core competencies of a company. PRAHALAD and HAMEL identified core competencies of a diversified firm as a very important source for synergies.[96] These scientists focused specially on management skills. These so called capabilities are in general a very important source for synergies but as this book is focusing on R&D, it is important to note that synergies in R&D are in general

---

[88] See Reed/Luffman (1986), p.34; Kanter (1998), p.155; St. John/Harrison (1999), p.129.
[89] See Ansoff (1965), p.78.
[90] See Porter (1987), p.58.
[91] See Rühli/Sachs (2000), p.127.
[92] The arguments in research papers are not consistent. Some researchers only stress the occurance of scope economics, others however also argue for the case of scale economics. This book is following the later arguments as the joint use of resources clearly offers possible scale economics. See Baumol et al. (1982), pp.47.
[93] See Ensign (2004), p. 132 or Nayyar (1992), p.220.
[94] See Nayyar (1992), p.220.
[95] See Prahalad/Bettis (1986), p.496.
[96] See Prahalad/Hamel (1990), p.91.

based on intangible resources. This is strongly linked to the functional organisation of diversified firms into a corporate level, a BU level and a functional level.[97] According to this structure synergies in R&D, Marketing, Distribution and other functions basically occur on a BU-level while immaterial and material synergies appear on a corporate level besides financial synergies which will be discussed in Chapter 2.4.1.3 in more detail. On BU level BIBERACHER identified two possible synergies. These are on the one hand cost-oriented synergies and on the other hand performance-oriented synergies. An example for cost-oriented synergies in R&D departments is the integration of R&D activities with controlling concepts, marketing concepts to reduce costs and optimise customer orientation. An example for performance-oriented synergies is the introduction of a quality management system.[98] These synergies are not the main focus of this book. The following examples can clarify some potential synergies of R&D departments which are of central importance. The most important characteristic of the synergies focused on in this book is that they occur between related R&D departments. With growing intensity and wider research areas of separate R&D departments' additional technology potentials start to develop.[99] Another example is that knowledge spillovers between R&D departments but also other externals like universities, other industries, cities, firms or individuals are an important factor for synergies.[100] Therefore one important question to be discussed in more detail will be the question on which levels due to the relatedness of R&D departments synergies occur and what possibilities exist to measure these synergies or degrees of relatedness.

In this context it is important to mention that the relatedness of tangible and intangible resources and the tangible and intangible synergies overlap each other.[101] This general introduction on the synergy concept is supplemented by a detailed view on other motives for diversification which were worked out by researchers over the last years.

---

[97] See Biberacher (2003), p.64.
[98] See Biberacher (2003), pp.64-82.
[99] See Gebert (1983), p.75.
[100] See Audretsch et al. (2002), p.171.
[101] See Szeless (2001), p.33 and Chapter 2.1.

2.4.1.2 THE RBV ON THE SYNERGY MOTIVES OF DIVERSIFICATION

The resource-based theory described in chapter 2.3 is relevant for both, the single business firm and the MBF also the attributes described are applicable on all resources.[102] Hence it is important to introduce the conditions to be fulfilled by a resource according to current literature to achieve synergies. The attributes discussed here are also described in chapter 2.3.2. The attributes in order of appearance are specificity, external mobility, imperfectly imitable and imperfectly substitutable

Specificity

Diversified firms need resources which are easy to share or split up. In consequence the specificity should not be too high in order to use a resource in many BUs. Therefore tangible resources need the attribute to be physically portable while intangible resources need to be transferable, i.e. useful and applicable, between BUs.[103]

External Mobility

Although resources for diversified firms need to be portable and transferable within the MBF, it is necessary that these resources can not be transferred easily to competitors.[104] The situation for the tangible resource is obviously not very difficult as over-capacities are transferred on regular markets. This diversification is not advantageous for a MBF as only costs of diversification occur and no economies of scope are realised. Intangible resources like know-how behave the opposite direction as they can be defined as a public good.[105] The third resource type is for example the image of a firm which is also intangible and not transferable for obvious reasons.[106] Hence using intangible resources is almost always advantageous for MBFs. This is based on the high costs for external transfers (if possible).[107] The characteristics discussed in the two sections above are enough to deliver recognisable synergies. Estimating the degree of synergies needs some more attributes which will be discussed in the following paragraph.

---

[102] See Peteraf (1993), p.187.
[103] See Szeless (2001), p.36.
[104] See Peteraf (1993), p.188.
[105] See Szeless (2001), pp.37-38.
[106] See Dierickx/Cool (1989), p.1505.
[107] See Szeless (2001), pp.37-38.

Imperfectly Imitable and Imperfectly Substitutable

Limited imitability and limited substitutability are further characteristics which make resources valuable for a firm. Both are a sustaining competitive advantage. Another important point to mention is that many synergies are based on resources with these characteristics.[108]

These attributes of resources can lead to a competitive advantage and in the long run to a superior performance according to the RBV.[109] Hence it is a very strong motive to diversify in this way but there are still some more motives left which are also important to note.

2.4.1.3 FINANCIAL SYNERGIES

Over the last decades the structure of the financial markets changed and over time firms adapted to this new environment. They developed corporate banks which offered financial services for internal but also external use. This is especially true for large firms which are often largely diversified.[110] One example can be the automobile producers who have their own corporate banks like for example the Daimler Chrysler Bank or the Volkswagen Bank.[111] Hence synergies are existent due to the internal capital market of a diversified firm which offers more possibilities for an efficient capital allocation than the external capital market. In consequence the firms strengthen their position and reduce at the same time their dependence on the capital markets.[112] Another advantage of this internal capital allocation is the lower costs for controlling the cash flows and also the possibility to optimise the microcontrol of the cash flows.[113] Besides the advantages there are still some critical arguments to be mentioned. On the one hand the advantages are weakened as the external markets adapt their efficiency to the internal markets. On the other hand an agency-theory based problem occurs which will be briefly discussed in chapter 2.4.2.2.[114] Strategic management scholars state that financial

---

[108] See Markides/Williamson (1996), p.341.
[109] See Wade/Hulland (2004), p.108.
[110] See Bank/Gerke (1998), p.31.
[111] More Information about the service and product portfolio of these corporate banks can be found under www.volkswagenbank.de and www.daimlerchrysler-bank.com.
[112] See Witte (1995), p.66.
[113] See Ganz (1991), p.78.
[114] See Szeless (2001), p.46.

synergies are of minor importance, as no firm would diversify just to achieve these synergies.[115] In consequence this book will ignore financial synergies as they do not help to meet the formulated objectives.[116] Another final reason for diversification is delivered by the managerial theories which are briefly discussed in the following paragraph.

2.4.1.4 MANAGERIAL MOTIVES FOR DIVERSIFICATION

The Principal-Agent Theory delivers another possible motive to diversify. Managers try to maximise their personal income and in consequence their personal power and recognition through the sheer size of a firm.[117] This theory was enhanced by JENSEN who published the so called free cash flow theory which also supports the idea that managers invest cash-flows into less profitable projects just to improve their power and not to distribute a dividend to the owners.[118] Besides the synergy motive there are as many theories on the motives of diversification developed as different scientific disciplines exist.[119] The following section is focusing on the most important theories from a market-based point of view, but also from a financial, managerial and behavioural point of view.

2.4.2 OTHER MOTIVES FOR DIVERSIFICATION

2.4.2.1 THE MBV ON THE MOTIVES OF DIVERSIFICATION

Structure-Conduct-Performance-Paradigm

The first motive for diversification is based on the Structure-Conduct-Performance-Paradigm. It assumed a strong connection between the market structure, the market behaviour and the market results.[120] The influence on the motives of diversification is twofold. On the one hand an attractive industry can form an incentive for firms to diversify into this market.[121] As criteria to choose such a market LÖBLER identified three criteria: a low degree of diversification, a forward-

---

[115] See Biberacher (2003), p.65.
[116] Scott (1977), pp. 1247-49.
[117] See Amihud (1981), p. 605.
[118] See Szeless (2001), pp.46-47.
[119] See e.g. Limmack/McGregor (1995), p.181.
[120] Cf Chapter 2.2.
[121] See Szeless (2001), p.41.

looking technology and high growth rates.[122] On the other hand firms can try to influence the structure of their industry to optimise their position within the industry. This can for example be achieved by a vertical integration.[123]

Market Power

A second motive is the market power which can be achieved through diversification. Scholars and managers developed two core strategies to exercise market power. One mechanism is the so called predatory pricing. Another possibility is the strategy of reciprocal dealing.[124] *Predatory pricing* describes a behaviour which leads to prices which are even lower than the marginal costs and in consequence lead to a crowding out of weaker opponents.[125] One necessary requirement is that cross subsidization between BUs of the diversified firm is possible. As the empirical tests do not give a clear statement whether the outcome is positive or negative the practical use can be questioned.[126] *Reciprocal dealing* is the second possible mechanism which can only be achieved through the market power of a firm. This expression describes the use or even the misuse of the market power by extorting suppliers or purchasing firms. One example can be that several BUs cooperate with one firm which in consequence depends to a large extent on the diversified firm. Therefore they have the market power to negotiate advantageous treaties for their BUs. Similar behaviour based on a supply and demand relationship of a diversified firm are especially the exclusivity of supply relations or bundling sales.[127] Another possible motive for diversification was developed by finance specialists. Therefore the following paragraph will pick up this motive and give a brief overview on this area of research.

2.4.2.2 RISK DIVERSIFICATION

This motive of diversification was basically developed by financial scholars.[128] The main argument of supporters of this theory of risk diversification can be summed up by three arguments. The diversification of a firm leads to more sustainability for

---

[122] See Löbler (1988), p.23.
[123] See Szeless (2001), p.41.
[124] See Ramanujam/Varadarajan (1989), p.535.
[125] See Montgomery (1985), p.790.
[126] See Grimm (1986), pp.71
[127] See Szeless (2001), p.42.
[128] See Gerke/Bank (2003), pp.52-53.

a firms operating profit. This can be revealed by reconsidering different seasonal, cyclical or structural changes in demand on different industries, countries or continents.[129] At the same time there are strong arguments against this theory of risk diversification. Especially against the background of the shareholder value discussion the objective of the traditional risk diversification can be achieved much easier and more efficient by the private investor themselves.[130] Also important to note is that empirical results suggest that diversifying firms destroy value instead of creating value.[131] Nonetheless there are three starting points which can lead to a positive outcome of risk diversification. These approaches generate value through the reduction of the unsystematic risk.[132] This brief survey on the three possibilities which reduce the unsystematic risk can give an insight on possible motives on diversification.

The *first possibility* reduces the unsystematic risk of agency-costs through the solution of the investment problematic which occurs through high volatile cash-flow profiles.[133] Due to volatile cash-flows there are two problems occurring as the owner does not know whether the investment is necessary or whether it is only a decision to fulfil the power ambitions of the management. On the one hand the cash flow is invested into unprofitable projects or on the other hand there is no money available for necessary and profitable investments.[134] Hence a constant cash-flow can reduce the unsystematic risk of this problem.[135] The *second possibility* reduces the unsystematic risk, if agency-costs[136] are existent as a consequence of moral hazard. Hence the cash flows of a diversified firm are much more constant because of the reasons mentioned above and are in consequence a better fundament for incentive schemes.[137] The *third possibility* is the reduction of the unsystematic risk of bankruptcy which was addressed by LEWELLEN. This theory is based on the broader capital base of a diversified firm and in consequence the possibility to increase the debts and therefore the firm's relevant

---

[129] See Gebert (1983), p.57 and Döhmen (1991), p.165 and p.201.
[130] See Hungenberg (2001), pp.398-399.
[131] See Gerke/Bank (2003), p.53.
[132] See Szeless (2001), p.43.
[133] See Stulz (1990), p.4 and p.16.
[134] See Berger/Ofek (1995), p.41.
[135] See Stulz (1990), p.4 and pp.16.
[136] For more information on the agency problematic see Jensen/Meckling (1976).
[137] See Marshall et al. (1984), p.2.

profit for taxation is reduced and leads finally to a higher value.[138] This theory was analysed and criticised by many scholars, but finally there is no clear answer on the influence of the firm value possible. Instead SCOTT stated that the risk of bankruptcy should not be a ratio to measure the value of a diversified firm. The literature also states that diversification does not only cause positive effects.[139] Reasons for these observed negative effects of diversification are also known as dissynergies and will be in the centre of the following section.

2.4.3 NEGATIVE EFFECTS OF DIVERSIFICATION AND DISSYNERGIES

One problem which already occurred with the positive effects was the problem of how to quantify these effects. This problems remains with the negative effects and some authors even state that it even is much more problematic than with the positive effects. Especially as scholars and managers underestimated or even ignored the negative effects.[140] PORTER identified three possible costs of sharing an activity due to interrelationships or diversified firms:

- The *costs of coordination* between two BUs involve at least personnel, time and potentially money. The costs will change depending on different environments; especially complexity and specificity are influential.
- The *costs of compromise* depend on the consistency of activities performed. These costs are the higher the less the activities are consistent. This means that activities cannot be performed as efficient as before due to the interrelationship of two or more BUs.
- The *costs of inflexibility* have two forms of manifestation. Firstly possible difficulties in reacting on changes in environment or competition and secondly exit barriers might hinder firm behaviour.[141]

Actual literature is more concerned about the negative effects of diversification.[142] This leads to the second problematic area, corporate culture, which can lead to

---

[138] See Lewellen (1971), p.521.
[139] See Porter (1985), pp.331.
[140] See Biberacher (2003), p.54.
[141] See Porter (1985), pp.331-335.
Note: Porter relates the costs to the material interrelation of activities.
[142] Cf Szeless (2001), p.48 and others.

dangerous culture shocks and even barriers to change.[143] In consequence it is necessary to be aware of these phenomena to react on possible problems. This means that only an active management of synergies can lead to the expected returns.[144] Another interesting insight is that with growing size the requirements on managers rise and parallel to the size also the complexity expands.[145] A final remark on the identification and implementation of synergies seems to be important. It is obvious that many firms identify material synergies but at the same time they do not identify immaterial synergies.[146]

Summarising the second chapter leads to three central points to be noticed at this point. First the explanation of diversification might be optimised by focusing on the relatedness of BUs within a MBF especially as the success of a firm can be explained by relatedness empirically and not as tried for a long time by the diversification itself. A second point to be noted is that the resource based view offers a static but nonetheless more precise view on relatedness than the MBV. Finally the motives for diversification show that synergies reflect a strong motive for diversification where relatedness seems obviously to play a role but which part is not clear yet and is going to be examined in the empirical part B. The following chapter is focusing on R&D as a very important function of today's firms. It is therefore fundamental to develop a scheme for theory and practice which helps to identify potential opportunities. This can be achieved by the resource based view introduced before. Beforehand it is necessary to develop a good understanding of the corporate function R&D which will be in the centre of the following part.

---

[143] See Frommann (2002), p.54 or Biberacher (2003), p.54.
[144] See Biberacher (2003), p.54
[145] See Szeless (2001), p.49.
[146] See Prahalad/Hamel (1990), p.79.

3 RESEARCH AND DEVELOPMENT IN THE FIRM

Analysing diversification and the impact of related R&D requires necessarily a detailed view on R&D itself. After the theoretical framework of this book has been outlined above, the following chapters will provide such in-detail analysis. In a first step, the relevance of R&D for corporate performance will be outlined, followed by a detailed structure of R&D activities.

3.1 THE RELEVANCE OF R&D FOR THE FIRM

Firms are acting within a continuous changing environment. Therefore, entrepreneurs have soon realised the relevance of innovation for their success.[147] On a larger scale, scholars today widely acknowledge the importance of technological change for economic development.[148] SOLOW argued, following the Austrian school[149] in Industrial Economics, that technological change is the primary determinant of economic growth.[150] The Industrial Research Institute stated in its Position Statement on U.S. Economic and Technology Policy in 1996 that during "the past 50 years, technological innovation has accounted for at least half of the economic growth in the United States."[151] SCHUMPETER contributed in this context meaningfully to the scientific discussion dealing with economic change. He stated in his work *Capitalism, Socialism and Democracy*:

"The essential point to grasp is that in dealing with capitalism we are dealing with an evolutionary process... Capitalism... is by nature a form or method of economic change and not only never is, but never can, be stationary. And this evolutionary character of the capitalist process is not merely due to the fact that economic life

---

[147] See Brockhoff (1992), p. 9.
[148] See Rosenberg (1994), p. 9.
[149] The Austrian School in industrial economics neglects the traditional static view on the market process and emphasised a market dynamics view. This school of thought originated during the 1870s with Carl Menger. Popular scholars following this approach were e.g. Ludwig Mises and Friedrich Hayek. Especially Joseph Schumpeter is usually linked with the Austrian School, see Jacobson (1992), p. 784. Theses economist are often described as the theoretic basis for modern strategic research and for e.g. for the work of Rumelt (1984) and Porter (1990).
[150] See Solow (1957), p. 312.
[151] Industrial Research Institute (1996) quoted in Wolff (1996), p. 3.

goes on in a social and natural environment which changes and by its changes alters the data of economic action". [152]

Being able to adapt to future developments is the key factor for economic performance of corporations. This causal connection is also shown, in a different field of research, by the design of many models measuring shareholder value. Nearly all of the relevant measures are based on the same underlying assumptions – "that price is the present value of expected future net dividends discounted"[153] at the cost of capital. To contribute to this future value of the firm is the central task for the R&D process within the corporation. R&D is able to contribute meaningfully to the future success of firms through the foundation of sustainable competitive advantage.[154] Hence, expenditures on R&D are positively acknowledged by capital markets. KOTHARI, LAGUERRE AND LEONE analyse the treatment of R&D expenditures in recent literature and state that empiric research illustrates "that on average the market assigns a statistically and economically significant valuation to corporate R&D activity."[155] Therefore, R&D is one of the key elements to generate future benefits. New applications for knowledge and the development of new products, services and processes is not only necessary to enable future growth but also for maintaining the actual business in relation to the life-cycle of single products.[156] Figure 3-1 outlines an example of a product portfolio to maintain the level of revenues over the life cycle of different products.

---

[152] Schumpeter (1943), 82.
[153] Lundholm/O'Keefe (2001), p. 311.
[154] See Yeoh/Roth (1999), p. 637.
[155] Kothari et al. (2002), p. 357.
[156] The life cycle phenomenon is, of course, not limited for product application, but also for whole industries. The life cycle concept is following the logic of birth, growth, maturity and decline based on a biological analogy and has found a wide acceptance. See Day (1981), p. 61.

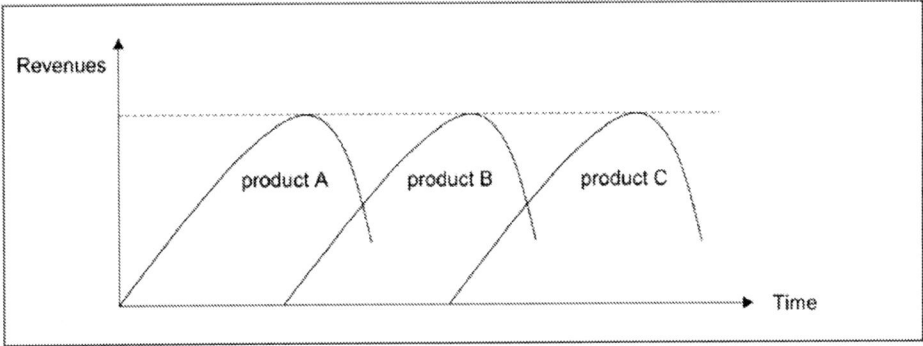

Figure 3-1 The life cycle and product portfolios
Source: based on Klepper, (1996), p. 562.

In order to be able to generate sufficient revenues and profits, a firm has to adapt its product portfolio continuously. Maintaining the competitive capability requires the steady development of new products, services and processes. To achieve this task, a continuous flow of inventions and innovations is mandatory. THOMAS A. EDISON described this target with the operation method of his laboratory where he tried to achieve "a minor invention every ten days and a big thing every six months or so".[157] This quotation describes the necessity of continuous professional corporate R&D for the future economic performance of the firm.

3.2 CLASSIFICATION OF R&D

R&D reflects the vague definition of research and development. The boundaries are indistinct and the literature often does not use a unique interpretation of the term R&D.[158] This book, however, tries to analyse the application of resources in R&D and therefore relies on a structured classification of R&D. The following section outlines the relevant aspects of R&D for the subsequent analysis.

3.2.1 TYPES OF R&D

Analysing R&D requires an investigation of the term "research and development". The following chapter is going to provide such a classification of R&D to enable

---

[157] Josephson (1959), p. 133
[158] See Sauer et al. (2005), p. 1.

profound descriptions of the underlying resource base and possible arising synergies. R&D itself and the R&D process can be structured in various ways. One of the most commonly used descriptions has been provided by the OECD with its Frascati Manual. Also every published approach can be criticised for its logic, this book will be following this R&D classification as the Frascati Manual has been used by the majority of R&D related papers[159] and therefore represents the standard in R&D surveys worldwide.[160]

The OECD defines R&D as following:

"Research and experimental development (R&D) comprise creative work undertaken on a systematic basis in order to increase the stock of knowledge, including knowledge of man, culture and society, and the use of this stock of knowledge to devise new applications."[161]

In this context R&D covers the areas basic research, applied research and experimental development.[162]

Basic Research is "experimental or theoretical work undertaken primarily to acquire new knowledge of the underlying foundations of phenomena and observable facts, without any particular application or use in view."[163] Basic research usually is performed by the public sector with institutions in the higher education sector but also by the government sector. However, meaningful private basic research efforts have to be acknowledged. The research on fuel cell is in this context an example to mention.[164] A further segmentation in basic research is possible with the separation of oriented basic research from pure basic research. Oriented basic research is expected to produce a broad base of knowledge likely to build the basis for other fields of application, whereas pure basic research contains research efforts without the attempt to apply the results to practical problems.[165] Basic research usually represents the pure scientific analysis

---

[159] Evangelista et al. (1998), p. 312.
[160] OECD (2002), p. 3.
[161] OECD (2002), p. 28.
[162] See OECD (2002), p.28.
[163] OECD (2002), p. 77.
[164] See Steinemann (1999), p. 3.
[165] See OECD (2002), p. 78.

published in public available literature. The results also contribute to an open discussion between interested scholars. Only rarely, basic research might be classified. This might happen e.g. in military industries.

Applied Research similarly to basic research attempts to acquire new knowledge; it is, however, directed towards a specific objective. It is undertaken either to specify the findings of basic research or to develop specific knowledge to solve predefined problems. In the private sector, basic research is often marked by the exploration of basic research results in order to create new and promising projects.[166] The results of applied research should be recognised as being applicable either only for one or a small number of products, processes or services. These results might directly lead to a patent process and usually are not a matter in public scientific discussions.

Experimental Development comprises, according to the Frascati Manual, the "systematic work, drawing on knowledge gained from research and practical experience that is directed to producing new materials, products and devices; to installing new processes, systems and services; or to improving substantially those already produced or installed."[167] Experimental development of services, related to the area of social science is, according to the manual, often further defined as the translation of knowledge accessed through research into operational programmes and final service offers.

However, in practice the categorisation of R&D is not always as easy to achieve as shown in the OECD Frascati manual. Basic research, applied research and experimental development is often performed within the same facilities and basically executed by the same staff. Also research projects might include activities, which straddle different categories. These operational problems have to be recognised during the later on following analysis of related R&D synergies.[168]
Table 3-1 shows the composition of these different R&D types for the U.S. for a period from 1990 throughout until 1998 to highlight the different relevance of R&D

---

[166] See OECD (2002), p. 78.
[167] OECD (2002), p. 79.
[168] See Evangelista et al. (1998), p. 312.

types in terms of spending. The figures shape the relevance of development spending for the private sector.

	Basic Research	Applied Research	Development
1990	4.6	22.6	72.8
1991	6.8	23.7	69.6
1992	6.2	22.4	71.4
1993	6.3	21.1	72.6
1994	6.3	19.9	73.8
1995	5.0	21.9	73.2
1996	5.7	21.0	73.4
1997	6.6	22.3	71.2
1998	8.1	19.2	72.8

Table 3-1 Percentage composition of R&D expenditure of the US economy

Notes: Company and other (except Federal) funds in the U.S.[169]

Industry funding is accountable for 69 percent of total R&D spending.[170]

Source: own calculations based on National Science Foundation, Basic Research and Applied Research by Industry, various years.

Traditionally, R&D research focused on manufacturing industries, if measuring private R&D spending. However, today's modern economies more and more can be classified as service economies especially as services are becoming the dominant part in contributing to national gross domestic products (GDP). This development clearly influences the financing and the actual performance of research projects. Comparable to manufacturing industries, the lion's share of R&D spending in service industries also accounts for experimental development.[171] The discussion of distinguishing between services and manufacturing R&D remains useful, is still ongoing. This paper is going to analyse R&D in common on an abstracted level and therefore does not distinguish between different industries, but focuses on private R&D in general. However, as

---

[169] The presented figures are based on data from the U.S. as comparable data for Germany or Europe have not been available.
[170] See Jankowski (2001), p. 323.
[171] See Jankowski (2001), p. 323.

many service industries lack a clear definition of corporate R&D substantial industries (e.g. banking, insurance, trade) will not be analysed during the empirical survey in the second part of this book.

3.2.2 INNOVATION AND R&D

R&D itself has to be recognised as a part of a larger innovation process.[172] R&D efforts are only a small contribution within the process from the basic project idea to the final innovation. R&D is a central, but nevertheless not the only component of the innovation process. It also has to be recognised, that in the linear innovation model, market reactions have to be acknowledged. Competitors are going to adapt new technologies if they turn out to be successful. EVANGELISTA et al. point out, that this adoption and diffusion of new techniques and processes is the basis for up to 50 percent of corporation innovation costs through the investment in machinery and equipment. R&D activities are also a central innovation activity accounting for only 20 percent of innovation spending.[173] These figures, however, vary for different industries and are just representing the average of a sample of European firms. The figures are also significantly correlated with firm size. Larger firms tend to be more R&D intense than smaller ones, what has been the key issue for a whole research discipline within industrial economics.[174] DEL CANTO and GONZALEZ summarised the relationship between innovation and R&D quite clearly:

"There are many ways through which firms can carry out innovative activities, on the one hand, through continuous internal investments [in R&D], ... [on] the other hand, firms may adopt the technology developed by other industries through external sources."[175]

This book is not going to address the discussion of innovation and firm size any further and just wants to highlight the wide area of different approaches on this particular topic. As a result, this book is going to analyse R&D for its resource

---

[172] See Evangelista et. al. (1998), p. 312.
[173] See Evangelista et al. (1998), p. 332.
[174] See for example the discussion in Cohen/Klepper (1996).
[175] Del Canto/Gonzalez (1999), p. 891.

relatedness and possible synergies and is not going to concentrate on an analysis of the whole innovation process.

3.2.3 BOUNDARIES OF R&D

Defining R&D properly raises several problems. Especially finding the right borderline of activities that should be included in R&D or not. This distinction is necessary to address R&D properly. In the context of related scientific areas a clear separation of R&D and other activities seems almost impossible. The Frascati manual clearly describes certain areas, which should not be part of measured R&D and can be summarised as follows.[176]

- Education and training of personnel and staff should not be included in R&D
- Related scientific and technological activities e.g. technical personnel, bibliographic services, patent services or the organisation of scientific conferences should not be included in R&D
- Other activities like related innovation activities e.g. the acquisition of technology or production related activities should not be included in R&D
- Administrative and general support activities e.g. human resource departments or central finance are not classified as R&D. However, these activities will be included within R&D expenditure, if these costs are included under overhead burdens

The authors of the manual also stress that this definition might not always be applicable. However, they try to present a pragmatic approach, which is useful for surveys analysing R&D.

Summarised the boundaries of R&D can be described as follows:

"If the primary objective is to make further technical improvements on the product or process, then the work comes within the definition of R&D. If, on the other hand, the product, process or approach is substantially set and the primary objective is

---

[176] See OECD (2002), p. 30.

to develop markets, to do pre-production planning or to get a production or control system working smoothly, the work is no longer R&D."[177]

This classification of R&D and its boundaries is going to build the fundament of the following analysis of the R&D process, the underlying resource base and the rising synergies.

3.3 R&D ORGANISATION

To structure the R&D function itself and to investigate the underlying resource base, it seems necessary to develop a profound understanding of R&D within a firm. The structural organisation of R&D has extensive impacts on the R&D process itself as well as on the success of R&D projects.[178] The analysis of R&D in this context has to acknowledge different perspectives on R&D organisation. However, the existing literature seems to agree on one thing: "There is no such thing as the best organisational structure for R&D and innovation."[179] Therefore, this chapter aims at outlining the wide field of possible organisational perspectives. This might be helpful to understand the strategic choices on R&D available for companies.[180]

3.3.1 FUNCTIONAL ORGANISATION

The implementation of R&D within the company has been the underlying object of several different organisational trends. To develop an in depth knowledge of R&D, its organisation and the relevant resource base, it seems necessary to recognise different modes of R&D organisations. In 1991, ROUSSEL et al[181] and ROGERS[182] in 1996 outlined different levels or generations in the progress and organisation of corporate R&D. This work outlined three (ROUSSEL et al.) respectively five (ROGERS) generations in R&D organisation. Although this

---

[177] OECD (2002), p. 42.
[178] See e.g. the work of Pike et al. (2005), p. 113, or the arguments presented in Teece (1986), p. 223. The impact of R&D organisation on the process an the success of R&D will be further analysed in chapter 4.
[179] Gilsing/Erken (2002), p. 11.
[180] See e.g. Volberda (1998), p. 67.
[181] See Roussel et al. (1991).
[182] See Rogers (1996).

formulation of general R&D organisation generations cannot be applied for all industries and corporations, they represent global trends in R&D strategy, as "there are a variety of 'in-between' options available".[183]

Since the 1960s R&D organisation departed from the traditional "stand alone" practices where R&D departments where functionally isolated and had been assigned to the common overhead.[184] This so called first generation model of R&D principally comprises to "hire good people, provide them with the best facilities money can buy, have them work in a 'creative' – possibly remote – setting, leave them alone, and hope they produce commercially viable results."[185] This form of R&D organisation, however, produced no sufficient R&D performance. For efficiency reasons from the 1960/70s onwards firms linked their R&D departments with the rest of business functions. R&D had been managed on a project-to-project basis and later on within an R&D project portfolio[186], describing the second (ROUSSEL et al.) and third (ROGERS)[187] generation of R&D organisation.[188] R&D departments had been structured as a matrix within the corporation. This project/portfolio strategy nevertheless had not improved the work of R&D departments even with increasing R&D spending.[189] In the light of the growing relevance of modern information and telecommunication technology both authors followed the next generation of R&D organisation. Intra-company organisation has to proceed further with the integration of R&D departments into the operative businesses. This generation has to integrate R&D, corporate strategy and the management of BUs entirely. The increasing relevance of information and knowledge causes ROGERS to outline a knowledge-based integration and management of R&D departments within enterprises. Knowledge related flows of information have to be organised as symbiotic networks to enable "knowledge

---

[183] Narula/Duysters (2004), p. 200.
[184] Rogers (1996), p. 36.
[185] Roussel et al. (1991), p. 6.
[186] See Canner/Mass (2005), p. 18.
[187] Rogers separates in her outline of R&D generations the project-to-project structure from R&D portfolio strategy, see Rogers (2005), p. 36, whereas Roussel et al. are describing a combined project based portfolio strategy, see Roussel et al. (1991), p. 7.
[188] See Rogers (1996), p. 37.
[189] See Canner/Mass (2005), p. 17.

processing capabilities that learn and feed forward intelligence to all participants in the R&D enterprise"[190]

3.3.2 GEOGRAPHIC ORGANISATION

3.3.2.1 INTERNATIONALISATION OF R&D

Corporate R&D is becoming increasingly internationalised. MBFs do not only diversify in terms of markets and products but also geographically.[191] In this context, the internationalisation of R&D is a popular issue in strategic management. KHURANA concluded that "it is clear that globalization of R&D is one of the key strategic decisions that almost every company – domestic or multinational – has to make."[192] This process can be observed since the mid 1980s when Dutch and Swiss companies subsisted, for the first time, more R&D sites abroad than inside their home countries.[193] Firms conduct R&D on a global scale mainly to access technology (e.g. via the acquisition of innovative firms)[194], markets or proximity to manufacturing locations.[195] COOK summarised the international perspective of corporate R&D quite clearly:

"Innovation is a global game – both on the supply side and on the demand side. You can't leave a technological window open in another geographical marketplace. ... If you want to lead with a new technology, you have to lead everywhere"[196]

This argument is quite strongly related with the underlying technology base. BARTLETT and GHOSHAL described the relevant market for micromechanics and electronics during the 1980s and found that "no single market could generate the revenues needed to fund the required state-of-the-art skills."[197] The location of R&D functions on sides abroad clearly opens a new variety of strategic choices. However, as GASSMANN and VON ZEDTWITZ point out, the increasing

---

[190] Rogers (1996), p. 37.
[191] See Gerybadze et al. (1997), p. 25.
[192] Khurana (2006), p. 49.
[193] See Gassmann/von Zedtwitz (1998), p. 147.
[194] See Gassmann/von Zedtwitz (1999), p. 233.
[195] See Khurana (2006), p. 49.
[196] Taylor (1990), p. 106.
[197] Bartlett/Ghoshal (1998), p. 26.

The missing central supervision might lead to unfocused research efforts and inefficiencies through parallel developments.[211] A characteristic example of the problems arising from such strategic organisations can be found with the development of a polymer through Royal Dutch Shell during the 1980s and 1990s.[212] The same product had been developed independently in three different R&D sites. The product only became an economic success after the assignment of responsibilities to a single R&D centre and focusing the efforts on market development.[213]

R&D Hub Model

To address the possible problems arising from ethnocentric and geocentric orientation, centralised firms often build an R&D hub model to structure their international R&D units. Although foreign R&D sites focus their research on predefined areas, they still remain under tight control from central R&D.[214] The corporation centre coordinates these decentralised R&D activities on a global scale. This structure enables the avoidance of redundant R&D projects as well as the usage of local knowledge and R&D resources. Therefore the R&D hub allows the generation of synergies arising between different sites. Nevertheless, this organisation requires high coordination efforts, causing high costs and consuming time. In addition, too tight central control might lead to the suppression of creativity and flexibility of local R&D teams.[215] In this context, KUEMMERLE points out that regional R&D units have to be organised in a way that ensures they operate above the critical mass to be able to fulfil their R&D tasks. On the other hand, under R&D hub organisation, R&D sites have to be small enough not to develop autonomous R&D activities.[216] Common examples for this organisational structure are Sharp and United Technologies where the main R&D site is located next to the corporate centre.[217]

---

[211] See Gassmann/von Zedtwitz (1999), p. 239.
[212] The product has been withdrawn from the market and is no longer commercially available as soon as early 2000, see Caulfield et al. (2001).
[213] See Gassmann/von Zedtwitz (1999), p. 240.
[214] See Lam (2003), p. 677.
[215] See Gassmann (1997), p. 336.
[216] See Kuemmerle (1998), p. 119.
[217] See Gassmann/von Zedtwitz (1999), p. 243.

Integrated R&D Network

This structure is seen as the most advanced R&D organisation where R&D sites are evolved into interdependent R&D units that are closely connected by multi-dimensional coordination and information links.[218] The domestic R&D department is no longer the centre of control. The developed network between R&D sites, however, prevails in the negative aspects of decentralised organisation forms. Single sites are assigned for the global responsibility for different technologies or products. These departments are developed as competence centres for their special research activity. This organisation form therefore bundles the positive effects of specialisation and local strengths. Nevertheless, this structure increases coordination costs significantly. Especially, the rising complexity of institutional rules and decision processes might be seen as a major drawback of this approach.[219] The competence centre model, which can be described as a lead-country approach, is the mainly used structure of US and European multinationals. Especially, pharmaceuticals usually position their R&D departments as international research networks.[220]

3.3.3 R&D COOPERATION

The R&D process itself has not to be restricted on corporate R&D. Cooperation with different external partner is a major factor in R&D.[221] HENDERSON and COCKBURN stress that knowledge flows across the boundaries of the firm and across scientific disciplines lead to more efficient R&D efforts.[222] For the sake of this analysis of R&D it is necessary to acknowledge possible cooperation and collaboration within the R&D process. However, the literature on cooperation in R&D is quite broad. The relevant scholars are from industrial economics[223] as well as from strategic management.[224] Therefore, this book is just presenting a brief summary of the ongoing discussion on R&D cooperation.

---

[218] See Lam (2003), p. 677.
[219] See Gassmann (1997), p. 337.
[220] See Lam (2003), p. 696.
[221] See Fritsch/Lukas (2001), p. 297.
[222] See Henderson/Cockburn (1994), p. 63.
[223] See e.g. Audretsch/Feldman (1996), p. 630 or Belderbos et al. (2004), p. 1237.
[224] See Quelin (2000), p. 476.

Firms "are aware of the necessity to establish R&D cooperation to obtain expertise which can not be generated in-house."[225] Such cooperation projects are more or less durable constellations of agreements between two or more partners to develop new or improved products, technologies or services.[226] Joint R&D seems to be of growing importance, especially within technology driven industries.[227] Even for large MBFs, collaborations in certain sectors can be useful to utilise external resources in order to realise e.g. technological opportunities.[228] Within R&D cooperation, different types of partners can be recognized. Literature usually separates three classes. Firms can collaborate with (1) competitors (horizontal), with (2) suppliers and/or customers (vertical) and with (3) universities and other research institutions (institutional).[229] A quite vivid example is given by Novartis Institutes for Biomedical Research, which is the global research organisation of Novartis in this field. This division operates more than 400 collaborations with both biotech companies and academic centres.[230]

Cooperation on R&D can be a major source for the realisation of synergies and can contribute meaningfully to corporate performance.[231] The main arguments for R&D cooperation usually are:[232]

- Cost/Risk sharing
- Access to technology and know-how in order to keep up with pacing development cycles
- Efficiency gains, e.g. economics of scale, scope as well as reduced uncertainty
- Competitive considerations, e.g. monitoring and influencing of partners
- Political considerations, e.g. subsidies, anti-trust[233]

---

[225] Becker/Dietz (2004), p. 209.
[226] See Becker/Dietz (2004), p. 209.
[227] See OECD (1998), p. 16
[228] See Arona/Gambardella (1994), p. 91.
[229] See Belderbos et al. (2004), p. 1237.
[230] Novartis (2006).
[231] See Prahalad/Hamel (1990), p. 80.
[232] Narula gives quite a broad literature overview on R&D cooperation and strategic considerations, see Narula (2003), p. 8.
[233] See e.g. Veugelers (1998), p. 420, Becker/Dietz (2004), p. 211.

It seems to be obvious, that MBFs can internalise some of these competitor-related arguments within their corporation. However, as mentioned earlier, the internalisation of functions always has to consider the legal environment (especially anti-trust) as well as the trade-off between dissynergies and the high risk of failure.[234] A high rate of MBFs operate cooperation agreements in R&D and are therefore able to benefit from joint programs and spill over effects.[235] Hence, cooperation in R&D has to be acknowledged as a relevant factor.

Summarising the gained information there are three core elements to be acknowledged. Firstly the significance of R&D for service industries similarly to the manufacturing industry is important to be noticed. This supports the choice of this book of focusing on R&D as a very important function within firms and leads to the second relevant element which defines the relevant activities in R&D for this book. Pointing out that this book is focusing on private R&D in general without a special industry focus and the belonging boundaries. This R&D consists of basic research, applied research and experimental development. At this point R&D is one element of the innovation process. Finally there is a strong influence of the organisation of R&D on the realisable synergies and other positive effects due to cooperation or relatedness of R&D. Nonetheless this book is not going to focus the analysis on the impact of organisational structures on the success of R&D in the empirical analysis, especially as the focus of this book is on measuring the resource relatedness of R&D. This seems to be necessary, as the ongoing discussion about R&D organisation, as outlined above, is vast and still growing. Hence, this book would not be able to include an adequate discussion about this field of research within the predefined objectives. Therefore the theoretical framework developed in this chapter builds the foundation for the classification of the relevant resource base in R&D and possible synergies occurring with these resources. This discussion is in the centre of the following chapter four.

---

[234] See Veugelers (1998), p. 420
[235] See Fritsch/Lukas (2001), p. 298.

4 SYNERGIES ARISING IN RELATED R&D

The origin of the analysis of synergies has to be built on the underlying resource base. The literature on relatedness usually focuses on specific resources and applies the analysis of these resources on the firm in general or on lines of business in detail.[236] FARJOUN analysed human experience as a relevant resource on industry groups.[237] A different approach on assessing relatedness focuses on the assessment of specific resources. Papers to point on, concentrate on advertising relatedness,[238] technological relatedness,[239] marketing relatedness,[240] manufacturing relatedness[241] or R&D relatedness.[242] However, these studies outline the topic from a general point of view. A quite common example for this global analysis had been shown by SILVERMAN. He compiled his investigation of technological resources through patent data. In this paper the number of patents represents the firm's available technological resources.[243] There are three logical counterarguments for this kind of analytical approach to be pointed out. The first one is the undifferentiated database, the second one the compiled dimensions of relatedness and the third one is performance effects. Hence, this book follows a different view on relatedness analysis instead. The underlying resources of single corporate functions are quite vast. In the following, the whole resource base of a single department (R&D) is going to be analysed. This approach tries to reveal synergies between R&D units and provides a detailed view into the relevant resource structure. This sight should help to understand relatedness as one of the main sources of synergies.

4.1 RESOURCES IN R&D

In the following chapter, this book develops a detailed resource concept, applicable for R&D departments, regardless of industry impacts. This will lead to a more aggregated level of resource description in general. Nevertheless, this

---

[236] See e.g. Tanriverdi (2005), Tanriverdi/Venkatraman (2005) or Farjoun (1998).
[237] See Farjoun (1994), p. 185.
[238] See Chatterjee/Wernerfelt (1991).
[239] See Robins/Wiersema (1995).
[240] See Capron/Hulland (1999).
[241] See John/Harrison (1999).
[242] See Chatterjee/Wernerfelt (1991).
[243] See Silverman (1999), p. 1113.

resource concept will still be applicable for empirical testing, as the single resources will be operational through development of more detailed sublevels.

A usual distinction of resources can be made with the separation between tangible and intangible resources.[244] A quite extensive structure of resources in R&D has been presented through PIKE et al... They distinguished human capital, organisational capital, relational capital, physical capital and monetary capital.[245] Often authors differentiate financial or monetary resources as a separate kind or resources.[246] In general, this approach seems to be quite useful as shown in the work of LONG and RAVENSCRAFT.[247] However, financial resources, especially in R&D, can be seen as unspecific resources. Cross-business relatedness on the basis of financial resources therefore cannot be interpreted as a major source of potential cross-business synergies.[248] Also the study by DEL CANTO and GONZALEZ leads to the result that "financial resources are shown to be hardly relevant."[249] Following this logic, this book will not separate financial resources as already introduced in chapter 2.3.1. Nevertheless, it has to be acknowledged that financial resources can act as barriers of entry for corporate R&D units and therefore influence the R&D behaviour of firms. The effects and implications are, however, out of the scope of this book and will not be investigated any further.

4.1.1 RESOURCES AND CAPABILITIES IN R&D

Despite the traditional approaches to innovation and R&D in the context of diversification,[250] the RBV enables an insight into the internal attributes. These characteristics are usually referred to as resources and capabilities as described above. These capabilities can be interpreted as bundles of integrated skills which are the result of collective learning of organisations.[251] This capabilities discussion focuses therefore on a more dynamic perspective: the development of skills useful for an efficient application of a specific resource base. This research school seem

---

[244] See Tanriverdi/Venkatraman (2005), p. 98.
[245] See Pike et al. (2005), p. 113.
[246] See e.g. Del Canto/Gonzalez (1999), p. 894.
[247] See Long/Ravenscraft (1993), p. 119.
[248] See Tanriverdi/Venkatraman (2005), p. 97.
[249] Del Canto/Gonzalez (1999), p. 903.
[250] See Cohen/Levin (1989), who provided an extensive review on this research approach.
[251] See Del Canto/Gonzales (1999), p. 894.

to explain a quite significant amount of diversification and resource efficiency. However, at any given point in time, these capabilities can also be interpreted as firm specific resources, e.g. the specific knowledge of certain employees. This book follows in its analysis a more static point of view. Hence, "a firm's resources at a given time could be defined as those (tangible and intangible) assets which are tied semi-permanently to the firm"[252] Therefore, the resource based view will not need to consider a distinction between resources and capabilities.[253] In the sense of this approach, this book follows the work of FARJOUN and structures the relevant R&D resource base into tangible and intangible resources.[254] This concept enables this analysis to cover 'soft' assets like knowledge as well.

4.1.2 THE RELEVANT RESOURCE BASE OF R&D

The structure of the relevant resource base of R&D is necessary in order to follow the basic objectives of this book: the development of a measurement concept of resources relatedness in R&D. This target requires a profound understanding of the relevant resources in R&D.

To structure the relevant resources within R&D, this book is going to follow STIER's framework for the developing of category systems. The formal requirements for this framework are as following:[255]

- Principle of comparability
  Each category and its sublevels have to be related to only one dimension in order to ensure comparisons within this class

- Principle of classification
  The categories and sublevels have to be mutually exclusive to enable a distinct classification

- Principle of completeness
  The category system as a whole has to be exhaustive, i.e. every possible element has to be classifiable

---

[252] Wernerfelt (1984), p. 172.
[253] See Wade/Hulland, (2004), p. 109.
[254] See Farjoun (1998), p. 612.
[255] See Stier (1999), p. 164 for an outline of the described system.

- Principle of independence

  All categories have to be independent from each other, i.e. the classification of single elements must not to affect the classification of other elements

This book is going to develop the resource base for R&D according to this framework. In this context, the structure of resources will build on the basic distinction of tangible and intangible resources without mentioning financial resources.

4.1.2.1 TANGIBLE RESOURCES WITHIN R&D

Tangible resources are the most exhaustively researched part within the resource-based school and dominated empirical investigations of this particular field of research.[256] Although tangible assets usually represent an important factor for the generation of synergies in manufacturing environments through scale economics, recent research papers point out the relative small impact, compared with intangible assets.[257] Nevertheless, tangible assets can be of significant importance for the realisation of synergies in related R&D. Structuring tangible resources will lead to a differentiated view on the relevant resources. This book will separate general tangible resources from specific tangible resources.

General Resources

General resources are firm-wide resources, which are obviously used by R&D departments. These resources contain mobile and immobile resources, which can be found throughout the whole company. R&D units benefit from these resources through straightforward usage. These resources contain e.g. buildings or different overhead institutions.

R&D Resources

R&D specific resources have to be acknowledged separately. These compound of R&D equipment that is in explicit use through R&D units. However, this equipment also contains elements that can be used not only within R&D departments. To

---

[256] See Szeless et al. (2000), p. 2.
[257] See e.g. Del Canto/Gonzales (1999), p. 891 or the arguments presented in Prahalad/Bettis (1986), p. 490 and Prahalad/Hamel (1990), p. 81.

consider such parts of the resource base, this paper will summarise them as general infrastructure and encloses e.g. IT networks or electronic devices. As a counterpart on this general equipment, R&D-only infrastructure like laboratory inventory or even particle accelerators can be distinguished.

Another important part of R&D, summarised under tangible resources, is the R&D staff. The total headcount of R&D personnel often represent a critical factor, acting as a barrier to entry.[258] Therefore, the pure headcount of R&D staff acts as a proxy for the size of R&D units measuring the actual number of scientists necessary for an entry in a certain field of research. COCCIA followed in his studies that the R&D headcount and therefore larger R&D sites can be a necessary prerequisite for the reduction of X-inefficiencies.[259] These resources can be used by different R&D sites and therefore can be the source of synergies. The following figure visualises the structure of tangible resources relevant for R&D.

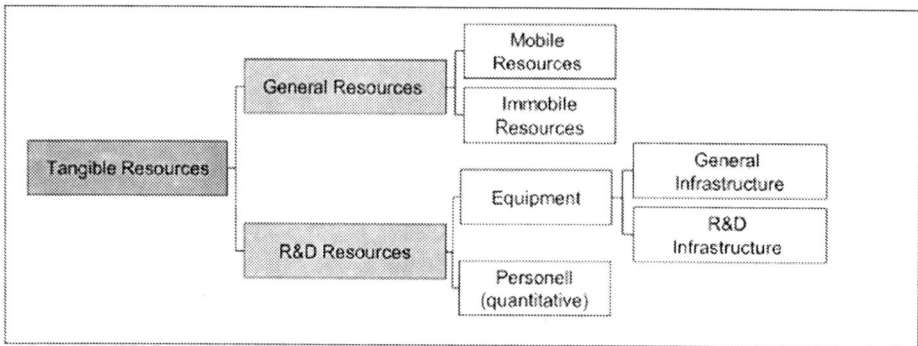

Figure 4-1 Tangible resources in R&D
Source: own development

4.1.2.2 INTANGIBLE RESOURCES WITHIN R&D

For a long time, empirical research focused on the measurement of tangible resources.[260] However, quite more important, especially in the context of R&D, it seems to be the acknowledgment of intangible resources. This statement can be

---

[258] See Hitt et al. (1990), p. 29 for arguments on the relevance of a critical number of scientists in R&D.
[259] See Coccia (2004), p. 267.
[260] See Szeless et al. (2000), p. 2.

followed from the vast stream of literature focusing recently on intangible resources within the RBV. Intangible assets seem to be more important from a strategic point of view as they are frequently outlined as a necessary requirement for the realisation of sustainable advantages.[261] The main argument in this context has already been outlined above: intangible resources are a higher potential source for sustainable advantages as they more easily fulfil the requirements to be valuable, rare, difficult to imitate and to be replaced.[262] One of the first authors to articulate the critical relationship was ITAMI in 1987.[263] TANRIVERDI and VENKATRAMAN rate intangible resources to be "more valuable".[264] A similar proposal can be found in DEL CANTO and GONZALEZ where intangible resources are stated to be "the most important ones from the strategic point of view".[265] Similar arguments can be found in the work of various other authors, e.g. in COLLIS and MONTGOMERY[266], GRANT[267], PRAHALAD and HAMEL[268] or PRAHALAD and BETTIS.[269] Especially the area of R&D provides a vivid example for the relevance of intangible resources. The research process can be classified as mainly knowledge driven and therefore offers a clear view on the meaning of intangible assets.[270]

The intangible resource base on a corporate level will usually be categorised into three main groups – human resources, organisational resources and relational resources.[271] This scheme includes the most commonly accepted categories.[272] However, in the literature a wide range of different classifications can be found. HALL divided intangible assets into intangible property, containing knowledge related legal rights, and intangible resources, summarising experience organisational structures as well as relation resources.[273] Another logic has been developed by EDVINSSON, who divided intangible capital into human capital,

---

[261] See Kostopoulos et al. (2002), p. 9.
[262] See also Leitner (2005), p. 128.
[263] See Itami (1987).
[264] Tanriverdi/Venkatraman (2005), p. 98.
[265] Del Canto/Gonzalez (1999), p. 896.
[266] See Collis/Montgomery (1998), p. 71.
[267] See Grant (1988), p. 639.
[268] See Prahalad/Hamel (1990), p. 79.
[269] See Prahalad/Bettis (1995), p. 5.
[270] See Koruna (2004), p. 506.
[271] See Pike et al. (2005), p. 112.
[272] See e.g. Bainbridge et al. (2001), p. 21.
[273] See Hall (1992), p. 135.

customer capital, process capital and innovation capital.[274] This book applies different views on the structure of intangible resources to develop a consistent resource scheme applicable especially for R&D units. This method distinguishes technology based resources and organisational resources.

4.1.2.2.1 KNOWLEDGE-BASED RESOURCES

Knowledge within the firm can arise in various ways. This book is going to structure this important resource according to the main focus of the analysed knowledge. Obviously, the most common interpretation of knowledge is technology related. However, as a counterpart, knowledge also is related with an efficient cooperation of personnel within organisations and therefore related with human resources.[275]

Nevertheless, a second important structure of knowledge has to be kept mind. Knowledge can be distinguished according to the accessibility.[276] On the one hand, knowledge can occur explicitly. Firms are able to rely on information from patents, copyrights, white papers or other forms of written down knowledge. This kind of knowledge offers easy access for the firm, as the corporation is able to use this knowledge regardless of the involved persons. On the other hand, knowledge can occur as tacit knowledge. A major part of the corporate knowledge resources is based on the available human resources as employees contribute their wisdom, experience and private information to their employer. However, this kind of knowledge is not always available for the firm and requires the collaboration of the relevant persons. Hence, this knowledge offers no easy access and is hardly to assess precisely.

This book is following the first distinction of knowledge for the development of the resource base as this represents a more functional structure. However, the second separation has to be kept in mind, as it is always necessary to value the analysed knowledge resource properly.

---

[274] See Edvinsson (1997), p. 320.
[275] See Teece (1986), p. 285.
[276] See Del Canto/Gonzalez (1999), p. 891.

Technological Resources

Technological Resources compile the knowledge on specific technological aspects. They also include technological understanding of the R&D staff which is accounted as technology specific. These resources can be distinguished according to their origin. External available resources include licences, i.e. technological wisdom available through the payment of fees as well as technological resources that can be available by cooperation with external partners. Joint programs between internal and external resources can contribute meaningfully to the quality and quantity of R&D processes.[277] These co-operations can be conducted with different partners. Possible external institutions are competitors (horizontal cooperation),[278] suppliers or customers (vertical cooperation) and scientific institutions like universities (institutional cooperation).[279] Firms are able to access key technologies and knowledge through cooperation. During this transfer process, firms have to be aware of the own technology base as well as of the level of external technology. Following this awareness, firms have to build up credible relationships with possible partners and have to be able to assimilate new technology inputs.[280] Besides this, technological resources are internally only available. This knowledge is based on the R&D process conducted within the different fields of basic research, applied research and experimental development. Firms often hold intellectual property rights which are certified (patents) or possess individual software systems.[281] R&D personnel contributes meaningfully to the internal available technology related knowledge through applicable knowledge based on education, skills and experience. This kind of intangible resources offer the technological framework for successful R&D efforts and qualifies the results of the firm's individual endeavours in basic and applied research and in development. Nevertheless, the relevance of technological resources varies between different sectors and industries.[282]

---

[277] See Koruna (2004), p. 506.
[278] See e.g. Sogaard (2001), p. 70.
[279] See Gilsing/Erken (2002), p. 23.
[280] See Lynskey (1999), p. 322, who gives an example of technology transfer within the IT industry.
[281] See Hitt et al. (1991), p. 695.
[282] See e.g. Pike et al. (2005), p. 113.

Human Resources

Human Resources compile key resources within the R&D process as researchers hold the personnel capability to process R&D projects. Human resources therefore are of crucial relevance for the corporate R&D resource base.[283] Highly educated scientists provide their individual knowledge, experience and abilities for the R&D process. They are therefore the key element for the realisation of R&D outputs.[284] However, this book will structure personnel knowledge related to specific technologies as technological resources. Apart from special knowledge, R&D staff possesses additional skills and capacities which have a strong correlation to R&D effectiveness.[285] R&D personnel can contribute to the R&D resource base through other hard skills which are not R&D specific, e.g. process management skills, product and market related knowledge or process knowledge. In addition available soft skills can foster the R&D process and therefore the resource base. These skills include communication skills, conflict management skills and the networking ability of researchers. This expertise seems to be of utter importance for the R&D efforts.[286] Various empirical studies seem to support the impact e.g. of communication on the results of R&D projects.[287] ALLEN states, that up to 40 percent of informal information-flows within R&D units lead to ideas considered during R&D projects.[288] These exchanges are "purely interpersonal (between individuals), ad hoc, and independent of organizational structure, policy, and formal collaborations."[289] Individual skills contributing to these collaborations therefore are key resources for corporations to use other R&D resources efficiently. Hence, this book will account individual skills as resources relevant for R&D.[290]

4.1.2.2.2 ORGANISATIONAL RESOURCES

Following a static approach in assessing R&D resources, as mentioned above, will classify organisational attributes of corporations as relevant resources. The

---

[283] See Bouty (2000), p. 50.
[284] See Souitaris (2002), p. 61.
[285] See Garcia-Valderrama/Mulero-Mendigorri (2005), p. 316.
[286] See Bouty (2000), p. 50.
[287] See Hirst/Mann (2004), p. 154.
[288] See Allen (1977), p. 45.
[289] Bouty (2000), p. 50.
[290] This conclusion can also be found in Markides/Williamson (1996), p. 340.

corporate environment, R&D units are embodied into, influence the ability to use existing resources efficiently and/or to access new resources. Hence, an efficient organisational structure can also be interpreted as a relevant resource for R&D.[291] These organisational aspects can be distinguished between resources related to structure and resources related to image and culture.

Structural Resources

The organisational structure of R&D units and the whole firm influences the performance of R&D processes. Especially in the light of increasing globalisation of R&D efforts, firms benefit from different internationalisation strategies.[292] The measurable trend for growing R&D internationalisation is mainly influenced through the occurrence of shorter product development cycles, global competition, increased customer expectations and technological risks.[293] In general, the organisational structure of R&D exercises a strong impact on the capability and performance of R&D. PEARSON[294] as well as DAMANPOUR[295] therefore categorised R&D organisational structure as a critical success factor. This structure can be further distinguished into aspects relating to the operational structure and elements connected to the organisational structure.

The operational part of the organisation's structure comprises the outline of the R&D workflow. This might include workflow management systems, knowledge management systems or the existence of formal committees. These systems regulate the actual workflow within R&D units and therefore directly operate the R&D process. Firms, which are able to create an efficient operational structure for their R&D activities, benefit from more efficient processes and therefore are able to create improved output from their R&D efforts.[296] Hence, operational structures should be recognised as possible resources within R&D units.

The organisational structure, on the other hand, describes the influence of corporate structure on the process of R&D. This structure comprises the

---

[291] See Markides/Williamson (1996), p. 346.
[292] See Kuemmerle (1997), p. 61.
[293] See Gassmann/Zedtwitz (1998), p. 147.
[294] See Person (1989), p. 87.
[295] See Damanpour (1992), p. 375.
[296] See Del Canto/Gonzalez (1999), p. 897.

hierarchical organisation, both within the R&D unit and firm wide. The organisational structure also defines the possible flow of information within the corporation and between different BUs and as well between different hierarchical levels. Hence, the organisational structure constructs the environment for R&D units and seems to be vital for capable R&D processes.[297] Also the structured relationship between R&D staff and corporate management affects the corporate capability to process R&D project and to develop future approaches.[298] Building a structure that fosters innovation can be a strong asset.[299]

Image

Another crucial resource is the perception of the firm. From an external point of view, the awareness of the firm can influence its ability to perform R&D projects.[300] This external awareness of the firm refers to corporate image or brand strength and can be interpreted as a resource within R&D. A positive external opinion can reduce corporate efforts e.g. for R&D staff assessment. Highly qualified scientists are more easily attracted by employers with a high image or popular brands. Other possible positive effects might be reduced search cost for future cooperation partners as such coalitions always are to some degree on a biased perception of reliance.[301] Also the process of gaining technology externally through licensing or acquisition can be positively related with the image of the acquiring firm.[302] Hence the reputation, brands and image can be described as relevant for the "suitable exploitation of R&D activities."[303]

Culture

Corporate culture refers to the culture and awareness of a certain firm towards R&D and innovation. TAYLOR states this relationship quite clearly with his "Business of Innovation" paper. In this interview PAUL COOK, former CEO of Raychem Corporation, outlines the necessity to involve top management into the R&D process. Managers have to "demonstrate genuine curiosity about what's

---

[297] See Harrison et al. (1993), p. 1031.
[298] See Szeless (2001), p. 150, who built this argument on the seminal work of Chandler (1962).
[299] See Taylor (1990), p. 98.
[300] See Del Canto/Gonzalez (1999), p. 897.
[301] See Veugelers (1998), p. 420.
[302] See Teece (1986), p. 294.
[303] See Pike et al. (2005), p. 113.

happening in the labs, it stimulates people to keep the creative process going."[304] On the other hand, scientists need to have the freedom to expand their own ideas in order to find real successful new approaches.[305] The culture may have a strong impact on the attitude of R&D personnel towards innovation.[306] The internal perception of firms within R&D units can contribute meaningfully to R&D quality and therefore should be regarded as a relevant R&D resource.[307]

Summarising the intangible resource base, applicable for R&D units, will lead to the following outline:

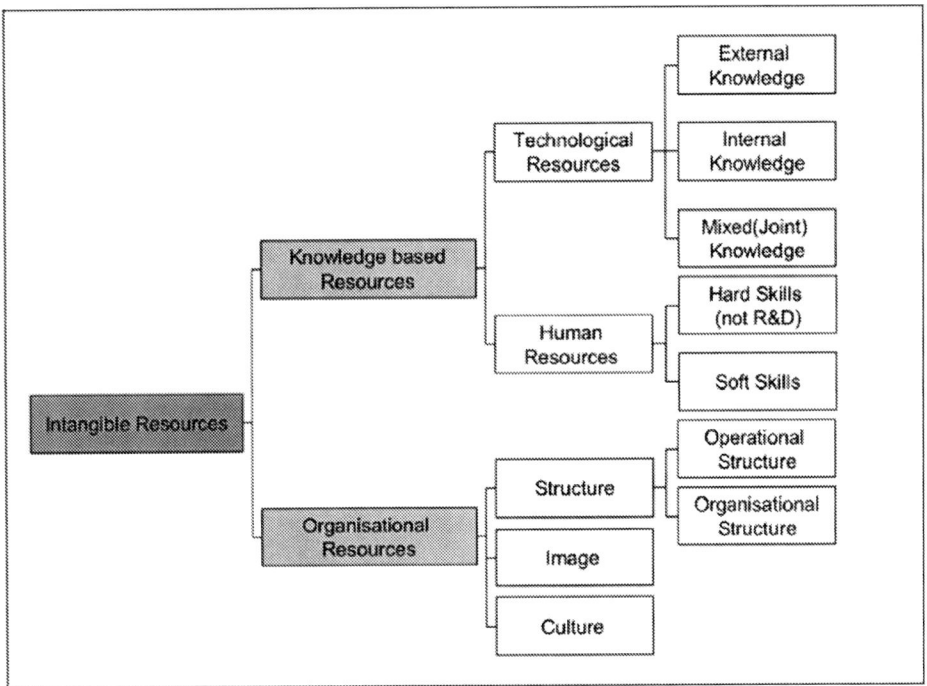

Figure 4-2 Intangible resources in R&D

Source: own development

[304] Taylor (1990), p. 98.
[305] See Quinn (1985), p. 77.
[306] See Garcia-Valderrama/Mulero-Mendigorri (2005), p. 316.
[307] See Pike et al. (2005), p. 113.

4.2 THE CONCEPT OF SYNERGY WITHIN R&D

Two different types of synergy effects can be distinguished in the strategic management and industrial economics literature – synergies arising from sub-additive costs and super-additive value.[308] Although this concept had been outlined above, this book will narrow this concept especially for the purposes of the analysis of R&D processes. This seems to be necessary in order to assess the concept of synergies completely. To avoid tautological problems arising from measuring synergies output-related as described by TANRIVERDI and VENKATRAMAN, this study relies on the assessment of synergies through the resource-based analysis.[309] Therefore, this book does not concentrate on synergies per se, but rather on the sources of synergies.[310]

4.2.1 SUB-ADDITIVE COSTS

This term refers to the commonly known economics of scope and scale as well as to increasing market power.[311] R&D units are able to generate synergies, if they use common factors within research reducing the costs of joint research activities.[312] This can be summarised to the following equation:

$$\text{Cost (R\&D unit 1, R\&E unit 2)} < \text{Cost (R\&D unit 1)} + \text{Cost (R\&D unit 2)}^{313}$$

This efficient use of common resources compels of course a common resource base of all participating R&D sites. R&D departments therefore have to be connected through related resources. Hence, resource relatedness captures efficiency gains through the sub-additive R&D efforts. This resource relatedness argument is following the RBV of diversification as in chapter 2.3. They are one major source for the creation of cost advantages or sub-additive production cost synergies.[314] However, the value of R&D within MBFs does not only compile from

---

[308] See Tanriverdi (2006), p. 59.
[309] See Tanriverdi/Venkatraman (2005), p. 99.
[310] Based on the concept of Davis/Thomas (1993), p. 1336.
[311] See Harrison et al. (2001), p. 681.
[312] See Teece (1980), p. 223.
[313] See Tanriverdi (2006), p. 59.
[314] See Robins/Wiersema (1995), p. 279.

pure cost advantages, but also from super-additive performance of related resources.

4.2.2 SUPER-ADDITIVE VALUE

In contrast to efficiency gains through sub-additive cost effects, a second synergy factor arises from the performance side of related resources. These super-performance results are mainly caused by spill over effects between a certain set of available resources.[315] The basis for this point of view can once again be found in the field of economic theory. Another important theoretical contribution has to be appointed to the literature on acquisitions and alliances.[316]

The returns of investments in R&D resources vary in the context of complementarity of the underlying resource base. "Complementary resources are not identical, yet they simultaneously 'complement' each other."[317] In other words complementary resources are distinct but nevertheless interdependent and mutually supportive.[318] A set of such R&D resources generates greater returns than the sum of the individual returns of single resources.[319] This connection can be reviewed with the following equation:

Return (R&D unit 1, R&D unit 2) > Return (R&D unit 1) + Return (R&D unit 2)[320]

Thus, complementary resources within R&D generate super-additive value synergies and contribute to the overall cross-unit performance of R&D departments. This book acknowledges complementarity effects as part of the traditional synergy effect, as complementarity seems to explain a significant contribution to the overall synergies arising from diversification. SONG et al. concluded from their appraisal of resource complementarity the following result:

---

[315] See Tanriverdi (2005), p. 313.
[316] Well-recognised authors in this field of research are e.g. Harrison et al. (2001) or Barney (1988).
[317] Harrison et al. (2001), p. 680.
[318] See Milgrom/Roberts (1995), p. 181.
[319] Tanriverdi (2005), p. 313.
[320] Based on Tanriverdi (2006), p. 59.

"Our research suggests that the synergistic performance impact of complementarity capabilities can be substantive in particular environmental contexts: while synergistic rents cannot always be obtained, it is possible to leverage existing resources through complementarity." [321]

Summarised, the underlying resources of R&D departments can contribute to two different scales to the return of R&D. First, related resources alter the necessary input contribution to R&D. Reduced research efforts are needed for the "production" of a given R&D result. Second, complementary resources contribute to the value generation of R&D. For a given R&D input, complementary resources generate improved R&D outcomes. Both effects have to be acknowledged during the analysis of cross-unit R&D departments. An easy example of multi-business R&D synergies can be structured as follows to highlight the two different effects. Two R&D units with the same strengths in basic research can obviously benefit from combined R&D infrastructure, e.g. laboratory capacities, and thus generate sub-additive cost synergies. R&D units with different strengths, e.g. basic research and development can benefit from each other's work to foster the own research projects. To enable this investigation a detailed view on relevant R&D resources seems to be of utter importance.

4.3 SYNERGIES ARISING FROM RELATED RESOURCES

The economic effects of related resources have been the scope of extensive research, both in empirical and theoretical papers. [322] The main argument for the benefits of related diversification has been argued in the ability to exploit economics of scope e.g. through shared facilities. [323] Benefits may also arise from e.g. better capacity utilisation and therefore generating economics of scale. [324] The complementary effects, as argued above, also might have an important impact on the generation of synergies through additional performance effects or economics

---

[321] Song et al. (2005), p. 259.
[322] See Hill et al. (1992), p. 502.
[323] See e.g. the arguments presented in Porter (1987), p. 43, Jones/Hill (1988), p. 159, or Teece (1982), p. 39.
[324] See Farjoun (1998), p. 614.

of time.[325] These effects apply to both tangible and intangible resources but to a different degree.

4.3.1 SYNERGIES IN R&D BASED ON RELATED TANGIBLE RESOURCES

Usually, tangible resources offer a wide range of potential synergies based on the joint use of R&D resources. On the one hand, general resources are most easily combined, as they are most unspecific.[326] Resources, classified as general infrastructure, clearly enable such joint use. As an example, combined IT networks can be leveraged on all corporate R&D sites. This behaviour might be a source for the realisation of economics and therefore synergies. Additionally, such resources can be the basis for the complementary use of other resources. IT networks can be the sources for inter company knowledge transfer.[327] On the other hand, specific R&D resources also enable joint usage. R&D infrastructure might be comparable across different R&D units. A possible example is the common use of exclusive analysis equipment, which can be used by different R&D units on different stages of the research process. Therefore, firms should be able to generate synergies through the realisation of different economies.

4.3.2 SYNERGIES IN R&D BASED ON RELATED INTANGIBLE RESOURCES

Similar economies might arise from related intangible resources. However, these synergies might occur in a different form as argued for tangible resources.[328] Intangible resources can be leveraged throughout the whole company not only through shared use, but also through the transfer of the intangible resources from one BU to another.[329] Thus this transfer might be even a more dominant source of synergies as the use of intangible resources is unlimited in the sense of resource capacity. Intangible resources usually do not possess a production limit. A quite obvious example might be the usage of registered patents. These should be acknowledged as intangible resources which can be used without limitations across the whole corporation. Transferable resources might offer specific benefits

---

[325] See Koruna (2004), p. 508.
[326] In general it has to be acknowledged that resource specifity and possible cross business use are negatively correlated, see e.g. Szeless (2001), p. 36.
[327] See Brown/Magill (1994), p. 176 and Tanriverdi (2006), p. 58.
[328] See Farjoun (1998), p. 614.
[329] See Tanriverdi/Venkatraman (2005), p. 100.

arising within a global R&D structure. In such situations, the leveraging of scientific and technical knowledge will be of special importance.[330] However, other intangible resources might exhibit constrains. An example might be tacit knowledge, related with R&D staff, and cannot be transferred to different BUs at the same time. This process might require the relevant person to contribute knowledge through workshops or individual meetings. Unless this knowledge is not contributed into a central database, access to tacit knowledge might be restricted. This example might be useful to point out possible dissynergies as mentioned earlier.

4.3.3 JOINT EFFECTS OF RELATED RESOURCES

The primarily described concept of complementary effects between different but interdependent resources seems to apply especially for resources within R&D.[331] The findings of FARJOUN appear to structure a similar approach. The unique set of resources offers the possibility to realise additional synergy effects.[332] This effect also has been described by KORUNA. The complete R&D environment therefore determines the possibility to accomplish the R&D projects successful.[333] Hence, the complete resource base of R&D units has to be analysed in order to appreciate all possible synergy effects of related resources. This approach should also address effects of differences in R&D inputs, caused e.g. through an internationalisation of R&D organisation.[334] As this book is going to outline the general impact of related resources in R&D, a really complete description of possible R&D synergies seems to be of no avail. Consequently, merely the wide range of potential synergies should be outlined. The OECD put this wide area of factors exerting influence on R&D in quite a vivid statement. "Successful R&D draws on ideas from many different sources, including informal professional exchanges, users' experiences and suggestions from the shop floor."[335] The global view on corporate R&D also enables a picture on synergies that are only apparent in this abstract view. KORUNA described these effects as "economics of

---

[330] See Khurana (2006), p. 49.
[331] See Cassiman/Veugelers (2002), p. 5.
[332] See Farjoun (1998), p. 619.
[333] See Koruna (2004), p. 514.
[334] See chapter 3.3 for more information on R&D organisation.
[335] OECD (1996), p. 32.

evolution"[336] in R&D.[337] The impact of such parameters had been shown through the possibility to compress the R&D learning curve.[338] Nevertheless, the description of positive effects from related resources should also include a depiction of viable negative effects occurring through the intended realisation of synergies.

4.4 DISSYNERGIES ARISING WITHIN RELATED R&D RESOURCES

As outlined above, synergies within R&D arise from the joint use or the transfer of resources across different R&D units. However, this combined usage might also cause negative effects. Above, dissynergies have been outlined in the approach of PORTER.[339] In R&D the attempt to realise benefits from related resources might face quite strong obstacles. However, synergy literature usually does not distinguish possible disprofits further and relevant papers do not apply them to single functional areas. The relevant literature usually focuses on the description of possible synergies and not on relevant dissynergies, see e.g. FARJOUN,[340] TANRIVERDI AND VENKATRAMAN[341] or PRAHALAD and HAMEL.[342] An exception might be seen in the work of KORUNA, who, however, focused on the capability of knowledge recombination only, and applied his findings on the analysis of certain case studies.[343] Hence, this book attempts to structure barriers to synergies more detailed for R&D. In order to present these problems more precisely, this book structures dissynergies into knowledge-based, cognitive and cultural.[344]

---

[336] Although the phrase "economics of evolution" is well known in economics literature, the application of this approach on the R&D process is quite rare.
[337] See Koruna (2004), p. 506.
[338] The possibility to compress the R&D learning curve had been empirically tested with positive results by the OECD in 1992.
[339] See chapter 2.4.4.
[340] See Farjoun (1998), p. 615.
[341] See Tanriverdi/Venkatraman (2005), p. 99.
[342] See Prahalad/Hamel (1990), p. 81.
[343] See Koruna (2004), p. 511.
[344] This book is applying the thoughts of Koruna (2004), p. 512 to structure the main areas of dissynergies applicable for R&D.

4.4.1 KNOWLEDGE-BASED DISSYNERGIES

R&D compiles, as conducted earlier, especially on scientific and technical knowledge. Diversified firms suffer with increasing diversity from a growing lack of awareness of their own resources.[345] Bearing in mind the complex structure of the resource base of R&D developed above, this argument seems quite obvious. The dispersion of knowledge, i.e. the widespread information of relevant resources across the firm, might therefore also prevent the joint use or the transfer of resources within diversified R&D projects.[346] Additionally, an increasing diversity among R&D units will be based on a growing diversity of the underlying scientific basics as well as between the relevant researchers. Hence, cooperation between R&D sites might be negatively correlated with differences between R&D projects.[347] To enable the realisation of synergies between such diversified R&D units might be difficult to achieve.

Similar problems might arise from the tacitness of knowledge. Frequently, specific knowledge is related to people. Hence, it might be difficult to assess, to structure and to transfer this wisdom for different R&D purposes.[348] Tacit knowledge reduces the possibility to use knowledge as an intangible resource across different BUs, although single R&D sites benefit from this asset.

4.4.2 COGNITIVE DISSYNERGIES

Cognitive dissynergies contain problems arising from interactions between R&D sites within a diversified firm. Different organisational trends might lead to the development of different communication schemes.[349] Especially widely diversified firms with decentralised R&D organisation might suffer from such communication problems between different sites.[350] Hence, growing diversity might prevent the realisation of synergies through related resources in R&D through growing communication problems between R&D units.

---

[345] See O'Dell/Grayson (1998), p. 11.
[346] See Galunic/Rodan (1998), p. 1193.
[347] See Brown/Duguid (1998), p. 101.
[348] See Koruna (2004), p. 511.
[349] See Boone (1997), quoted in Koruna (2004), p. 511.
[350] See Pfeffer/Sutton (2000), p. 9.

Related with problems of decentralisation might be the valuation of different resources. In order to point out relevant resources for cross-functional usage, single R&D units have to be able to acknowledge the individual relevance and value of resources. However, as diversified units might apply a different view on these assets, individual prejudices might prevent the efficient corporate wide use or transfer of resources.[351] Especially decentralised R&D departments might apply different views and valuation and a strong central synergy management might be necessary to outline possible approaches for R&D synergies.

Very closely connected to the appearance of cognitive dissynergies is the approach taken by the agency theory. The management of possible synergies will be conducted within the company by different agents. Obviously, these agents are influenced by their own position, capability and perception.[352] The possibility of the realisation of synergies therefore will be influenced by the bounded rationality of agents within the company.[353]

4.4.3 CULTURAL DISSYNERGIES

Apart from structural boundaries,[354] which can be a serious obstacle for the generation of synergies, cultural impacts can be the reason for major dissynergies. Diversification implies the cooperation of people with different backgrounds. R&D staff will include scientists from different scientific fields. R&D specialists have a certain understanding of their job and their own working culture what can lead to functional and personal differences between different kinds of scientists.[355] These differences might lead to communication problems between R&D personnel and hinder the common use of resources.[356] The necessary growing specialisation of researchers reduces a global understanding for the strategic corporate view. Specialists therefore are less able to understand meaning of cross-functional cooperation and are less able to accelerate joint use of related resources. They

---

[351] See Hargadon (1998), p. 209.
[352] A quite broad introduction into agency theory and bounded rationality of agents can be found in Rumelt et al. (1991), p. 5.
[353] See Fleming (2001), p. 117.
[354] The obvious problems arising are e.g. organisational differences and are described e.g. by Nayak/Ketteringham (1986), p. 13.
[355] See Koruna (2004), p. 511.
[356] See Leonard-Barton (1992), p. 111.

often suffer from a lack of ability to communicate properly beyond the boundaries of their own field of specialisation. Quite often, this problem will be described as the 'engineer syndrome'.[357] Hence, the generation of synergies, based on related resources, is decreasing with growing diversity.[358]

Another well-known problem arising in this context can be described as the 'Not-Invented-Here Syndrome'. It mainly describes the negative attitude of researchers on the application of externally developed knowledge and can be observed at many research laboratories.[359] Such behaviour will undermine the attempts to foster joint use and the transfer of related resources. Especially the knowledge driven R&D process might suffer from cultural dissynergies like the Not-Invented-Here Syndrome.

Summarised, the generation of synergies from related R&D resources will have to address major obstacles. These problems will reduce the benefit of synergies in the sense of PORTER and have to be acknowledged during the analysis of related R&D.[360] However, it seems quite obvious, that the described obstacles might also turn into influential assets, if the corporation is able to create a synergy friendly environment, e.g. through the development of a cooperative culture across different R&D units. Overall the described resource base can be taken as a general categorisation which can also be used for other functional areas with specific requirements like marketing or sales. These detailed categories are fundamental for further analysis and the development of a measurement system of relatedness. Also important to keep in mind are the occurring synergies and dissynergies bound to this resource base. This book is especially focusing on relatedness and in consequence on potential synergies. Hence the dissynergies are of minor importance for this book.

---

[357] See Koruna (2004), p. 511.
[358] See Argote (1999), p. 5.
[359] See Katz/Allen (1988), p. 3.
[360] See Porter (1985), pp.331-335.

5 THEORETICAL BASIS TO ANALYSE RELATEDNESS EMPIRICAL

Measuring relatedness and its correlation to performance is one of the most discussed questions in strategic management. Scholars conclude that related resources within a diversified firm lead to a superior performance.[361] Hence the discussion is manifold and needs a more detailed view on the empirical studies performed and the most important results on measuring relatedness over the last decades. This will be discussed in the first part of this chapter. Secondly it is important to discuss the analytical tools used to measure relatedness directly and indirectly. Direct measures are in the focus of the second part while indirect measures are in the centre of part three.

5.1 LITERATURE REVIEW ON EMPIRICAL RELATEDNESS RESEARCH

BETTIS suggested, based on two regression models that related diversified firms have performance advantages which are strongly influenced by expenditures in R&D.[362] There are numerous works supporting these performance advantages of related diversified firms through empirical evidence.[363] It is also important to note that there are also other empirical results which argue the opposite of the above studies[364]. One reason for these different results is offered by ROBINS and WIERSEMA who identify "weak conceptual grounding" and many untested areas.[365] These early scholars based their work on a more abstract relatedness of industries to each other.[366] This direction changed with some exceptions in the 1990's and focused on the single resources available in firms. [367] This shifting focus was accompanied by the assumption that cross-business synergies due to the relatedness and complementary of BUs lead to performance advantages.[368] Hence scholars tried to identify relatedness for several functions within a

---

[361] See Tanriverdi/Venkatraman (2005), p.97.
[362] See Bettis (1981).
[363] For more empirical evidence supporting the superior performance see Rumelt (1982), Palepu (1985), Varadarajan (1986), Varadarajan/Ramanujam (1987), Jose et al. (1986).
[364] For more empirical evidence supporting the inferior performance see Michel/Shaked (1984) or Chatterjee (1986).
[365] See Robins/Wiersema (1995), p.278.
[366] See Farjoun (1994), p.187.
[367] See Tanriverdi/Venkatraman (2005), p.97.
[368] See Tanriverdi (2005), p.313. for more information read also Chatterjee/Wernerfelt (1991), Markides/Williamson (1994), Robins/Wiersema (1995) and Farjoun (1994).

diversified firms (e.g. IT or Human Resources).[369] The first to be introduced was product relatedness. It was discussed by RUMELT (1974)[370] and furthermore by other researchers. Another important relatedness was investigated with customer relations.[371] This lead to an awareness about the importance of relatedness in general, but also about the product relatedness in particular.[372] One reason might be that these single resource perspectives are easier to observe, especially with continuous measures based on the SIC system.[373] The empirical problems of continuous measures by using the SIC system will be discussed in more detail in chapter 5.2.1. Consolidating the early empirical research on relatedness the focus on product similarities is obvious.[374] This changed among others with PRAHALAD and BETTIS publishing their ideas on managerial relatedness which suggested that a concept of "strategic similarities" might be developed to substantiate this relatedness.[375] Another empirical study performed by ILITICH and ZEITHAML delivered evidence that Galbraith's centre of gravity (1983) hypothesis as a managerial dimension of relatedness is more important than product relatedness in achieving high performance. This means that the relatedness of management reduces complexity and applies core skills appropriately". Even if this study found a negative correlation of product relatedness and a positive correlation of managerial relatedness to performance, the tenor is that there are still many unknown dimensions which might be very influential.[376] Two important functional dimensions were examined by CHATTERJEE and WERNERFELT in 1991.[377] This study tried to find out whether advertising intensity or R&D intensity is more significant for the performance of a firm. The results supported other researchers who suggested that R&D intensity is more important for a good performance than advertising.[378] Other dimensions which were discussed and analysed in the following years are the human resource relatedness which was discussed by FARJOUN in 1994.[379] This work proved that firms diversify into industries which

---

[369] See Tanriverdi/Venkatraman (2005), p.97.
[370] See for example Lemelin (1982)
[371] See for example Palepu (1985).
[372] See Lemelin (1982), p.655-656.
[373] See Robins/Wiersema (1995), pp.279-280.
[374] See Ilinitch/Zeithaml (1995),p.401.
[375] See Prahalad/Bettis (1985), pp.496-499.
[376] See Ilinitch/Zeithaml (1995).
[377] See Chatterjee/Wernerfelt (1991).
[378] See Chatterjee/Wernerfelt (1991), p.41.
[379] See Farjoun (1994).

are related in "types of human skills" and the "expertise" which is required in this industry.[380] Hence relatedness of human resource and human knowledge is another essential dimension to keep in mind. Important with this indirect measurement[381] is the introduction of occupational profiles.[382] A dimension of minor importance was identified by ST JOHN and HARRISON in 1999. They found no evidence that manufacturing relatedness leads to financial advantages for the multi business firm.[383] Other findings were published by CAPRON and HULLAND in 1999. They focused in more detail on the marketing expertise during horizontal acquisitions. Concluding that the likelihood of mobile resources to be redeployed is higher than it is for immobile resources. Also interesting was the finding that cost-based synergies were almost not affected while revenue-based synergies and the general firm performance were significantly influenced.[384] Finally after discussing the most important dimensions the empirical research on the area of R&D and technological relatedness which was already slightly touched earlier is going to be discussed in more detail. MONTGOMERY and HARIHARAN published their findings on the influence of R&D intensities, advertising intensities and capital expenditure intensities. One conclusion is that firms diversify in areas where similar intensities can be found and higher intensities lead to more diversification which was interpreted as a higher output of transferable resources which in consequence lead to competitive advantages.[385] Another approach was used by ROBINS and WIERSEMA who used a technology inflow-outflow matrix[386] to measure the relatedness of an industry. Finding that performance of firms diversifying in technologically related industries is better than the performance of firms which diversified in technologically unrelated industries.[387] The work published by FARJOUN displayed the multidimensionality of the relatedness concept. He identified a matrix of interrelationships across business segments consisting of activities (e.g. R&D) and resources (e.g. tangible and intangible).[388]

---

[380] See Farjoun (1994), p. 185.
[381] A more detailed analysis on measures of relatedness can be found in chapter 5.2.
[382] See Tanriverdi/Venkatraman (2005), p.98.
[383] See St. John/Harrison (1999), p.129.
[384] See Capron/Hulland (1999), p.41.
[385] See Montgomery/Hariharan (1991), p.
[386] Based on a development of Scherer, who combined information on patent filing with input-output data intending to construct a matrix of R&D flows between industries. For more information see Scherer (1982).
[387] See Robins/Wiersema (1995), p.292-293.
[388] See Farjoun (1998), p.626.

Using this classification, points out the strength and weaknesses of all the concepts of relatedness.[389] Summarising the literature discussed up to now there are two streams crystallising. On the one hand there are scholars basing their work on intensities and on the other hand there are researchers build their research on approximations which rely on the SIC system. In this context it is important to note that these works are mainly focusing on the industry relatedness of diversified firms.[390] As this book is focusing on a functional relatedness of BUs the importance of such measures is not as paramount as expected in the beginning.

The following scholars focused their attention more on cross-business synergies while still using slightly adapted instruments to measure relatedness. SILVERMAN for example based his work on patent data to explore the influence of the technological base of a firm on its diversification behaviour. Finding that firms diversify in areas where they can use their existing technological resources. Interesting is the developed measure of a firms technological resource base which can easily be linked to product markets.[391] Unlike SILVERMAN, TANRIVERDI who analysed Information Technology (IT) relatedness as a source of cross-business synergies and the question whether IT relatedness enables a multi business firm to use cross unit knowledge management capabilities which might affect the positive performance[392] of a firm. Empirical evidence lead to the suggestion that IT relatedness is important for knowledge management capabilities which are themselves important for the success.[393] One important improvement which can similarly be observed with the next paper is the direct measurement of relatedness by a questionnaire among senior IT executives.[394] This questionnaire also underlies the publication of TANRIVERDI and VENKATRAMAN which focuses on three types[395] of knowledge relatedness and possible performance improvements. The empirical results educe that a single related knowledge does not lead to an

---

[389] See Farjoun (1998), p.626.
[390] See Silverman (1998), p.2-5.
[391] See Silverman (1998), pp.22-23.
[392] Another important area of research is the influence of IT investments and their performance effects. KOHLI and DEVARAJ (2003) performed a meta-study to give an overview on the results of one decade and give implications for future research, but more details would lead too far.
[393] See Tanriverdi (2005), p.327.
[394] See Tanriverdi/Venkatraman (2005), p.98
[395] The three types of knowledge relatedness are: customer knowledge relatedness, product knowledge relatedness and management knowledge relatedness.

upgraded performance, but synergies which arose through the complementarity of the three knowledge relatedness improved performance significantly.[396] A similar modus operandi was taken by TANRIVERDI to investigate the IT relatedness and its relationship to the firm's performance. The finding is that the moderating force in this relationship is the degree of diversification.[397] This overview on empirical research points out that there are several areas which are still unexplored. One obvious problem is the investigation of single resources. This can be problematic especially as MBFs try to exploit cross-business synergies in different resources simultaneously. Hence treating these synergies as independent gives a high risk of inconsistent results.[398] FARJOUN expressed this problem as follows

"[...] empirical research has usually looked at how an individual resource or base of relatedness evokes a diversification pattern without regard to the interaction among several resources."[399]

These are the most important reasons for this book, investigating all possible resources[400] in R&D. Another important point to be recalled from this literature review is the fact that there was no empirical attempt made to measure relatedness in a single function. After reasoning about the results of the empirical research, another important question for further discussions is the way in which relatedness is going to be measured.

5.2 MEASURES OF RELATEDNESS

As the overview on the latest literature has pointed out there are several different approaches on measuring relatedness. The most important possible measures will be discussed in this chapter. Therefore strengths and weaknesses of these methods are pointed out intending to choose the best analysing tools available. On the one hand there are direct measures of relatedness which will be in the focus of chapter 5.2.1. On the other hand there are indirect measures of relatedness which will be in the focus of Chapter 5.2.2.

---

[396] See Tanriverdi/Venkatraman (2005), p.97.
[397] See Tanriverdi (2006), p.57.
[398] See Tanriverdi/Venkatraman (2005), p.98.
[399] See Farjoun (1998), p.612.
[400] Compare with chapter 2.3. and chapter 4.

5.2.1 MEASURING RELATEDNESS DIRECTLY

Measuring relatedness of a firms resources directly at the firm level was and is seen as being very difficult.[401] Performing a primary analysis or direct measurement makes the data ascertainment a central element of the measurement.[402] Nonetheless these direct measures of relatedness are applied several times over the last years especially by TANRIVERDI and his colleagues.[403] Reasons for the use of these direct measures are very simple, first scholars can precisely address the problems they want and collect the specific data they need. Another important advantage is that this data is up to date which is not necessarily given with secondary data.[404] Many of these advantages are at the same time disadvantages of indirect measures. This holds especially on the advantage that direct measures are closer at the resource base, so that they consider the underlying assets and resources.[405] In consequence these measures aim on actual relatedness while indirect measures aim on potential relatedness.[406] This difficulty of "potential relatedness" is explained in the following chapter 5.2.2. Besides this closeness to the resource base, it is also much easier to operationalise the data as it is specially designed for the purpose of this study. In consequence the results would have a higher validity.[407] Nevertheless measuring relatedness directly is seen as very difficult at a firm level mainly because of the many dimensions to be considered.[408] Another difficulty of direct measures is that there are always quantitative and qualitative criteria that need to be identified. This is especially difficult in the case of qualitative criteria.[409] There are also some more problems occurring by applying a direct measure, but as these are dependent on the methods, they will be discussed later. The description of these methods and the developed direct measurement will be discussed in chapter 5.2. Beforehand the indirect measures need to be explained in more detail to give an overview on possible methods used in the empirical analysis.

---

[401] See Tanriverdi/Venkatraman (2005), p.98.
[402] See Stier (1999), p.232.
[403] See Tanriverdi (2006), Tanriverdi (2005) and Tanriverdi/Venkatraman (2005).
[404] See Stier (1999), p.233-234.
[405] See Markides/Williamson (1996), p.363.
[406] See Tanriverdi (2005), p.98.
[407] See Tanriverdi (2005), p.98.
[408] See Markides/Williamson (1994), p.158.
[409] See Garvia-Valderrama/Mulero-Mendigorri (2005), p.311.

5.2.2 MEASURING RELATEDNESS INDIRECTLY

At the beginning it is necessary to explain what indirect measurement of relatedness means. Indirect is used to explain that the data which is used for the analysis is based on so called secondary data. This secondary data is not collected for the study itself but for example by the government or other institutions for statistical reasons. Hence the data collection is not specified for the purposes of an academic study.[410] Measuring relatedness "indirectly"[411] is one of the most popular approaches in the last decades of diversification research.[412] This can on the one hand be traced back to the difficulties in measuring relatedness directly[413] and on the other hand on the development of the available analysing tools as can be observed.[414] Another reason might be the possibility to access the data relatively easy in comparison to the direct measurement due to public databases using the SIC system.[415] Finally indirect measures deliver some objective data.[416] It is important to note that even if this measuring tool is very widespread there are also some negative points to be kept in mind. There are at least three main arguments criticising indirect measures.[417] First NAYYAR addressed the problem that indirect measures are far away from the reality. His argument is that this method can only measure a "potential" relatedness between two BUs which can be explained by the quality of the secondary data.[418] Potential relatedness is often equalised with actual relatedness which is not correct especially as advantages out of potential relatedness[419] are hard to realise.[420] This however leads to misunderstandings and inconsistent results of empirical works.[421] A second point of critique is brought forward by DAVIS and DUHAIME who state that tangible resources (e.g. production) are better captured than the intangibles (e.g. R&D, Marketing) which are not as completely and precisely reflected as the tangibles

---

[410] See Stier (1999), pp.232-234.
[411] Other expressions for indirect and direct measurement are for example „external" and "internal" used by Nayyar (1992),p.219, or "macro" and "micro" used by Robins/Wiersema (1995), p.292. This book will only use the expressions mentioned in the text ("direct" and "indirect").
[412] See Tanriverdi/Venkatraman (2005), p.98.
[413] See Tanriverdi/Venkatraman (2005), p.98 and for more information chapter 5.2.2
[414] See for example Farjoun (1994), Robins/Wiersema (1995), Silverman (1999) and others
[415] See for example Farjoun (1994), p.189 or Davis/Duhaime (1992), pp.513-515.
[416] See Tanriverdi (2006), p.63.
[417] See Tanriverdi/Venkatraman (2005), p.98.
[418] See Nayyar (1992), p.219.
[419] More information about realising potential benefits from relatedness can be found in Ansoff (1965) or Chandler (1962).
[420] See Reed/Luffmann (1986), pp.34-35.
[421] See Tanriverdi/Venkatraman (2005), p.98.

are.[422] A third critical comment suggests that these "traditional" measures only reflect an incomplete and disproportionate picture of the relatedness between single BUs.[423] The critique shows that there is the requirement to measure relatedness on a more detailed level to get more significant results. This short introduction with a brief overview on general strengths and occurring weaknesses should help to understand the different measurement methods developed over the last decades. Especially in the context of choosing the best indirect measure which can be a possible approximation of the later explained direct measured results.

5.2.2.1 CATEGORIAL MEASURES

These measures are based on the work of WRIGLEY and built on the typological (subjective) work which was pushed and finished by RUMELT in 1974.[424] This measure was very "judgemental" in its application, as it based on some strong assumptions. On the one hand researchers need a very detailed knowledge about each of the firms in terms of corporate structure; on the other hand they also need a complete knowledge of the different categories of relatedness to classify the firms correctly.[425] The main problem occurring due to this proceeding is the difficulty for other researchers to replicate the research especially as scholars determine relatedness as "weighted average of similarities".[426] Two decades of research brought controversial results with this measure but the bigger part challenged this method of measuring relatedness.[427] These circumstances lead to the search and development of more objective measures.[428] Hence this book will not revert to this method.

5.2.2.2 CONTINUOUS MEASURES

According to DAVIS and THOMAS several scholars suggested that continuous measures are in general very "mechanistic" in their application. One basic element

---

[422] See Davis/Duhaime (1992), p.521.
[423] See Markides/Williamson (1994), pp.149-150.
[424] See Ramanujam/Varadarajan (1989), p.539.
[425] See Robins/Wiersema (1995), p.278.
[426] See Davis/Thomas (1993), p.1336.
[427] See Robins/Wiersema (1995), p.279.
[428] See Hoskisson et al. (1993), p.216.

for the use of continuous measures is the assumptions concerned with the SIC, which suppose that "all relatedness is fully determined by a two-digit SIC".[429] This means simplified speaking that if the two-digit SIC is similar the firm is related and the other way round. Among scholars and researchers these continuous measures developed a very high popularity over the last years for several reasons. First, continuous measures offer a "higher level of measurement" and besides this a "wider range of techniques for analysis". Also very important is the use of "standard categories" for data. Finally research is "replicable" and "cumulative" and due to the SIC system it is possible to use a broad range of data available.[430] On the one hand the SIC code[431] brought more objectivity to the empirical relatedness research especially among Anglo-American researchers.[432] On the other hand it is at the same time one of the weakest links which will be highlighted through the following arguments. A fundamental critique was formulated by RUMELT who identified two weaknesses. First he highlighted the different extent of the SIC industry classifications and that this also leads to implicit industry classes. Even if the classes are carefully selected the implicit assumption of similar differences between these classes is problematic.[433] Another problem addressed by DAVIS and DUHAIME is the unsatisfactory coverage of non-manufacturing groups which need to be covered separately.[434] There are two more critical remarks by DAVIS and THOMAS. They criticise that the SIC bases only on production or output similarities to summarise businesses. Another argument is that there is only relatedness or synergy. Therefore no differentiation between different types of synergies is possible.[435] Further fundamental critique is formulated by SILVERMAN. He points out that it is not clear whether 3- or 4-digit SIC codes share "similar use patterns" or not. This relies on the fact that the SIC system is based on product characteristics which is similar to output rather than on resource characteristics which are equivalent to input.[436] This argument leads to the conclusion that all continuous measures based on the SIC system are too far

---

[429] See Davis/Thomas (1993), p.1337.
[430] See Robins/Wiersema (1995), pp.279-280.
[431] biotechnology has no own code yet. But nonetheless large German firms (DAX 100) are also given a SIC Code.
[432] See Markides/Williamson (1994), p.343.
[433] See Hoskisson et al. (1993), p.218.
[434] See Davis/Duhaime (1992), p.522.
[435] See Davis/Thomas (1993), pp.1337-1338.
[436] See Silverman (1998), p.3.

away from the resource base to measure it properly. Hence this book will base its indirect measure not on a database like this. For the high acceptance of the SIC system within empirical research one could say, among the blind the one eyed is king. This is probably the reason why continuous measures received so much confidence by researchers especially from the US. The confidence was also strengthened by an accurate and consistent definition of segments and professional reporting.[437] This, apart from some single exceptions in general, seems to be fulfilled and even if this book is not going to use the SIC systems to measure relatedness, it is necessary to shortly introduce the most important continuous measures. For the sake of completeness it is important to note that there is a comparable coding system in the EU which is called NACE-Code. This system has very similar problems and is also not complete; one example is that there are still no codes for biotechnological firms.[438] For simplicity reasons the two coding systems are assumed to be identical.

One basic work on continuous measures in diversification and relatedness research was – according to VILLALONGA – published by JACQUEMIN and BERRY in 1979.[439] One of the most often used measures for diversification and relatedness was the **Herfindahl Index**.[440] This appraise enables the researcher to capture the "relative importance" of BUs. This is achieved by taking all sales of one BU into consideration.[441] Hence this measure is able to assess the total and related diversification, but it can also assess intrafirm relatedness among BUs of the same industry.[442] The concentric index[443] and the entropy index[444] are two other measures which are in the centre of many empirical studies.[445] This **concentric index** is designed to measure to what degree relatedness contributes to the cross-business synergies all over the firm. It consists of the sales of a firm in different industries which are weighted by a variable weighting factor

---

[437] See Davis/Duhaime (1992), p.513.

[438] See Edler (2001), p.4.

[439] See Villalonga (2004), p.496.

[440] See Davis/Thomas (1993), p.1337.

[441] See Stimpert/Duhaime (1997), p.116.

[442] See Farjoun (1998), p.616.

[443] For more information see Montgomery/Hariharan (1991), "Diversified entry by established firms", in: Journal of Economic Behaviour and Organization, Volume 15, pp.71-89.

[444] For more information see Jacquemin/Berry (1979), "Entropy measure of diversification and corporate growth", in: Journal of Industrial Economics, Volume 27, pp.359-369.

[445] See St. John/Harrison (1999), p.140.

corresponding to the relatedness.[446] As the original index was also based on the SIC system there were several developments of scholars which tried to improve the estimation of synergies by implementing new data.[447] The second measure is the already mentioned **entropy index**. It is based on three elements, first the number of product segments, second the distribution of product sales across these product segments and third the degree of relatedness among the product segments.[448] A study performed by HOSKISSON et al. supported the reliability and validity of the entropy measure.[449] Nonetheless other scholars discussed the importance of these measures and the tenor is that serious questions about their validity are raised due to their limited information which is provided on the interrelationship of BUs.[450] The recognition of this circumstance in combination with the inherent problems of the SIC system led to further developments. In this context two approaches are necessary to be highlighted. The first is a continuous measure introduced by FARJOUN which was already addressed in Chapter 5.1. This was a new approach especially as it extended the used data also on non-manufacturing industries and used a broader base of information. Hence the economy was divided into "Resource-Related Industry Groups" which was defined as similarities at the human expertise.[451] This "structural equivalence modelling" was a big step especially as the used information had a stronger linkage to the underlying critical resources than the previous works had.[452] ROBINS and WIERSEMA developed an even more detailed measure which was based on a technological relatedness based on SCHERER's technology inflow-outflow Matrix.[453] One important finding is that this resource-based index of relatedness seems to be different from the classical entropy index or concentric index. They suggest that this measure is closer to the resource-based theory and therefore delivers more reliable results than other measures.[454] However, there remain some questions concerned with the applicability of these measures for non-manufacturing firms like discussed before. Another problem is that even if the

---

[446] See Robins/Wiersema (1995), p.280.
[447] See e.g. Davis/Thomas (1993), p.1338.
[448] See Palepu (1985), p.244.
[449] See Hoskisson et al. (1993), pp.232-233.
[450] See Robins/Wiersema (1995), p.281.
[451] See Farjoun (1994), pp.185-187, see also Coff/Hatfield (1995).
[452] See Robins/Wiersema (1995), pp.283-284.
[453] See Tanriverdi/Venkatraman (2005), p.98.
[454] See Robins/Wiersema (1995), p.293.

latest theories came closer to the resource-base there is still some distance left which is not solved yet. Especially important for this book is the fact that assessing relatedness of R&D is not possible with these measures as they are focusing on the relatedness of BUs which is not the main objective of this book with its functional approach and the focus on R&D. There are some more approaches which try to overcome these problems. They are discussed in the following paragraph.

5.2.2.3 OTHER MEASURES

The measures discussed before are obviously still characterising resources at the industry level and the BU level without focusing on functional relatedness. This leads to a lack of information especially on firms expertises. This problem was addressed by SILVERMAN, who tried to get closer to the resource pool of a firm by **patent count**.[455] This patent count does not share the same concerns about the explanatory power as the entropy or the concentric measures explained before.[456] Still problematic is the measurement of tacit knowledge as it "leaves no traces".[457] Despite this there is also the problem that the service or sometimes the software industry does usually not use the patent mechanism.[458] These industries use protection mechanisms like copyright and trademarks.[459] Thinking about the implications for this book there arise no consequences for the use of this indirect measure especially as among R&D departments the patent mechanism is very well established. Other phenomena like cross-licensing and patent pools can lead to biased results in patent count.[460] Another problem might be that from the sheer patent count there is no prediction about unique and specific or common and applicable use of patents possible.[461] It is also clear that some patents are more important than others which can not be reflected by counting them. Using patent count also underestimates the ratio of a firm with rapidly growing R&D as its results are based on earlier lower R&D expenses. Besides this there are also different time delays between the R&D expenditure and the result in form of a

---

[455] See Silverman (1998), pp.4-5.
[456] See Miller (2006), p.602.
[457] See Miller (2006), p.606.
[458] See Tanriverdi/Venkatraman (2005), p.98.
[459] See DTI (2005), p.73.
[460] See Grindley/Teece (1997), p.8 and 34.
[461] See Tanriverdi/Venkatraman (2005), p.107.

patent. These delays vary significantly between different industries.[462] These arguments show that there are still some critical points to keep in mind especially for a comparison of BUs acting in different industries, but in general it seems to be a concept which can be a good basis for further analysis if the necessary data is available.[463] Another important measure which is going to be discussed is the already introduced **R&D intensity** (Chapter 5.1). This is obviously an input oriented accounting based measure as it is commonly defined as "ratio of R&D expenses to sales in one period of time".[464] Some researchers suppose that measuring R&D intensity as R&D spending per employee is more stable.[465] A third definition is delivered by MILLER who measures R&D intensity as R&D expenses over total assets.[466] There are several more definitions used in literature.[467] Recognising these definitions this book will unless otherwise noted use the R&D intensity as ratio expenses to sales. The reason why it is possible to use this input based measure is delivered by ACS et al. who suggested

"that the innovative output of all firms rises along with an increase in the amount of R&D inputs, both in private corporations as well as in university laboratories".[468]

This finding explains very well why it makes sense to take this input based measure. Another advantage of R&D intensities is that they have empirically only little variation over time.[469] Hence a static analysis should be accessible with this measure.

The two measures discussed yet seem not to display all measures available that intend to measure output of R&D indirectly. Some more interesting outputs are discussed by VALDERRAMA and MENDIGORRI. They identified especially the publication of books and articles, development of software, product and or process

---

[462] See DTI (2005), p.73.
[463] In the US, patent data is very easy to access while in other countries this can be a problem
[464] See Chatterjee/Wernerfelt (1991), pp.38-39.
[465] See Barker/Mueller (2002), p.788.
[466] See Miller (2006), p.610.
[467] See for example Audretsch et al. (2002), p.182, where R&D intensity is defined as "R&D employees as percentage of total employees".
[468] Acs et al. (1994), p.340.
[469] See Siegel (1997), p.73.

innovation.[470] The problem of measuring these outputs is obviously the availability of data. Especially the product and process innovation is almost impossible to measure indirectly and even a direct approach will not always achieve reliable results.

This chapter is concluded by noticing that "traditional relatedness" researchers were mainly concerned with a general degree of relatedness between different BUs in different industries. In contrast to that direction this book is following a more functional approach by focusing on relatedness in R&D in single BUs. In the same moment it occurs that this relatedness is not gripped by the measures discussed before. In consequence it seems to be necessary to introduce a new measurement concept for this relatedness. Only knowing what resources are most relevant for R&D might lead to the relevant measures. Therefore measuring relatedness of R&D BUs seems to be the key for further analysis and a more detailed approximation than past research.

---

[470] See Garcia-Valderrama/Mulero-Mendigorri (2005), pp.312-313.

INTERIM CONCLUSION

Summarising the main function of Part A, it is to present the theoretical and practical fundaments for a complete and operational measure which is in the centre of discussion in Part B. Therefore the first part introduced the relevant expressions with an emphasis on the RBV which is the relevant perspective of this book and at the same time reflects the state of the art in diversification research. Also important is the awareness of scholars, that the success of a diversified firm can best be measured by its relatedness. Nonetheless there is no clear answer to the relatedness of BUs as there is no complete and integrated concept that reflects relatedness on the level of a function of a BU even if synergies are usually only occurring within and between these BUs.

Another important development of this Part A is the introduction and definition of an R&D concept which is building the base for the identification of resources and connected synergies. The last chapter of this first part is closing down the focus on the measures available in order to assess the characteristics of a more detailed and reliable relatedness measure. Most important as outlined is the awareness that indirect measures are usually only proxies for relatedness which can not be valued as the direct measurement does not exist so far on a BU level.

Describing this virtual measure of relatedness after this first part leads to a measure based on the resource based view. The measure should comprise the whole resource base of R&D or at least the most important resources identified by an empirical study. Also important is the question whether relatedness is closely connected to potential synergies or not. Besides this there are questions concerned about the identification of important or less important resources which is on a general level very difficult but at least the attempt should be made. Answering these two questions would offer the possibility to construct a relatedness measure that might be reliable in measuring relatedness directly. The development of a detailed questionnaire in order to measure the relatedness directly and answer the two questions introduced before is a section in Part B. Also contained within this questionnaire are questions dealing with the organisational structure and other questions of more general topics. This knowledge derived from the empirical analyses should then be used for the development and operationalisation of a measure of relatedness. The optimum would be to create a measure that offers one final number that tells the interested person about the degree of relatedness of the examined BUs R&D. Developing this measurement concept is the main objective of Part B but requires as explained a detailed analysis of the fundamentals.

INTRODUCTION PART B

This second Part B is based on the knowledge about relatedness measures developed and described before. The theoretical know-how is going to be empirically tested in order to use these empirical results for a more detailed direct measure of relatedness in a second step. The approach and the objectives of this second part B are graphically displayed in Figure 1-1b.

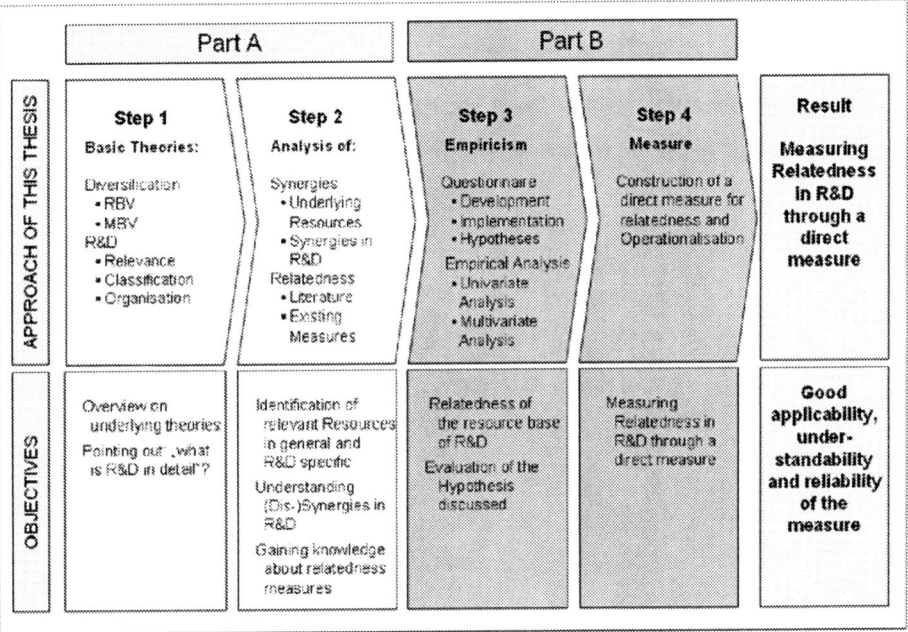

Figure 1-1b Overview on the Approach and Objectives of this book
Source: Own Development

Besides this figure a short introduction on the following chapters might be helpful to find into this book. The virtual relatedness measure and its characteristics described in the interim conclusion of Part A are in the centre of the development of the questionnaire. The core questions are based on the resource base identified before and try to measure resource relatedness, identify resources that are important for the success of R&D, and find out whether relatedness is the same as potential synergies. These questions are very interesting from a general point of view as they are closing a gap existing in relatedness research where no relatedness of resources on a BU function like R&D was measured yet. A by-product which is at least interesting but dependent on the results of the questions introduced before are the possible consequences for the resource base. Especially as the results might point out some specific resources which are more related than others. These resources could then be used to create a relatedness measure on a more detailed sub-level than the existing measures which are basically focusing on R&D intensities or patent counts measured indirectly or single resources measured directly. Therefore this book might provide a more detailed insight into the resource relatedness not only by identification of relevant resources but also by measuring these resources and their relatedness with a new measurement concept. Whether these ideas are realisable as explained before is going to be analysed in the following chapters.

6 MEASURING RELATEDNESS WITH AN EMPIRICAL SURVEY

Developing the measure of relatedness on a resource-base is something new to this area of research. Especially the concept of this book to measure relatedness for one complete functional area (R&D) and affiliated with that the complexity of resources which has to be covered in all possible dimensions has not been available yet. Hence it is necessary to introduce the basic objectives and general conditions of such an empirical evaluation. Besides this the questionnaire is introduced in detail.

6.1 BASIC PRINCIPLES FOR THE EVALUATION OF RELATEDNESS

This chapter can be divided into two separate areas. Firstly there are general objectives which should be met by this concept. These targets are closely linked to the basic assumptions and requirements which must be met by the measure explained in Part A. Additionally to these requirements there are a few objectives and general conditions surrounding the implementation and realisation process of this empirical survey. Finally the statistical background is introduced which is necessary for the following chapter.

6.1.1 DETERMINATION OF BASIC OBJECTIVES AND GENERAL CONDITIONS

In the beginning it is useful to sum up the most important aims of this book. On a very general level there is the need to measure relatedness in diversified firms with a special focus on the resource-base of R&D departments in different BUs (cf. chapter 5.2). A very basic objective of this measure is to identify possible resources which are related to each other (e.g. R&D specific infrastructure in BU 1 is related to the R&D specific infrastructure in BU 2). Another important goal – yet also one that is much more difficult to achieve – is to measure the degree of relatedness which might give some implications for the management especially in connection with arising synergies. One more potential aim is to identify the importance of single resources which might be possible. The following chapter will give a detailed introduction on the single dimensions that are used to meet these basic objectives. The introduction of the resource-base of R&D (cf. Chapter 4.2.), constitutes a very good theoretical framework for the development of relatedness measure.[471] An additional important objective is the closeness of the measure to the resource base in order to measure actual relatedness.[472] This focus would make the operationalisation much easier so that the identified resources are very close to the phenomena of relatedness.[473] But this strong concentration on one core function can be limiting.[474] Hence they are very close to the "construct" of resource relatedness. Besides these objectives for the direct measurement of resource relatedness this book is also aiming to find an approximation which can identify this relatedness measured directly from an indirect perspective or from a more detailed sub-level directly. In other words this book is trying to find some indirect measures like for example R&D intensity or other indirect criteria which might help to identify relatedness from the outside of a firm or split up the identified resources into more detailed sub-levels. Which concept is going to be realised will depend on several factors that are going to be discussed in more detail in the rest of this book. Further claims are of an empirical nature and aim on the description (descriptive analysis) of the current degree of relatedness of R&D departments. Alongside the hypotheses which are developed in chapter 6.2.3, should be verified.[475] Nonetheless a detailed description of the development process will be given in the following chapter. But first there are some basic principles derived from empirical and relatedness research that need to be fulfilled in order to construct a useful measure. Four formal requirements or principles for the analysis of a problem on the one hand and for the development of a measure on the other hand are mentioned by STIER. Firstly the "principle of comparability" anticipates that there is only one discussed dimension. This is obviously the case as the whole theoretical framework is based on resources. Secondly the single categories must exclude each other, taking the example tangible and intangible resources the excludability is clear. Thirdly there is the need for completeness which is a difficult principle in general. In the case of this theoretical framework it seems to be achieved on a concrete level as all possible resources available for a BU performing R&D are documented (cf. chapter 4.1.2). Finally the separate resources must be independent of each other. That means in detail that one

---

[471] See Miles/Huberman (1994), p.18.
[472] See Markides/Williamson (1996), p.363. For a more detailed picture cf. chapter 5.2.
[473] See Hübler (2005), p.39.
[474] See Miles/Huberman (1994), p.22.
[475] See Diekmann (2004), pp.31-33.

resource must not predetermine another one.[476] Hence the basic principles for the development of such a theoretical framework are fulfilled which is a necessary base for a maximum of reliability of direct measures of relatedness.[477] These general or formal requirements are complemented by some more specific requirements derived from the theoretical basis of relatedness, already discussed in detail in chapter 5. This brief overview on the most important underlying principles and objectives to achieve a good measure of relatedness shows that there are many sources of error during the development of a measure like this. In the following part the implementation and realisation of the measure in its fundamental structure is in the centre of discussion.

6.1.2 IMPLEMENTATION AND REALISATION

The first step to get a precise knowledge about the used method is to collect the essential data about the identified resources. Literature identified on the one hand the conduction of surveys and on the other hand a more experimental approach through observations or simulations.[478] Traditionally the most commonly used form of data collection is the survey. There are three different forms of performing the survey, per interview, telephone interview or questionnaire.[479] For this book the questionnaire is chosen with the intention to give a very detailed view on resource relatedness. This intention is supported by HÜBLER who suggests that the data collected by questionnaires are of higher quality than the data collected with other methods. Also important are some advantages compared with interviews. First the costs are much lower for a "mail survey", a second argument is the large number of persons that can be surveyed and finally the answers are suggested to be more "honest" and "deliberate".[480] While being aware that the efforts for a questionnaire are still relatively high and that nonetheless there is a high risk of a low rate of return, this book conducted a survey based on questionnaire.[481] Hence the development of a questionnaire started on the base of the resource framework

---

[476] See Stier (1999), p.164-165. These principles are comparable to the MECE-ness principle that is "mutually exclusive and completely exhaustive". More information about that theorem can be found in Hungenberg (2002), pp.22-24.
[477] See Stier (1999), p.51.
[478] See Bryman/Cramer (1994), p.3.
[479] See Hübler (2005), pp.42-45.
[480] See Stier (1999), p.198.
[481] See Hübler (2005), p.44.

developed in chapter 4.1.2. Developing the questionnaire started with the identification of the possible addressees which is a fundamental knowledge for the formulation and specification.[482] The target group include persons with the relevant knowledge about resources in R&D and the necessary bird's eye view on possible relations between similar resources. This respondent qualification leads to the target group which is in the best case a responsible manager from the board of directors or also possible an R&D senior executives of a diversified firm.[483] Before introducing the structure of the questionnaire it is important to make some general remarks on the wording and syntax used. The development of the questionnaire is based on clear and brief sentences with concrete, neutral, and simple wording as far as possible. Leading questions are also avoided like the unacceptable hypothetical questions.[484] Further potentials to distort the results of the measures are the formulation of the questions where incomprehensible, undifferentiated or equivocal questions may lead to wrong results. Similar problems occur if important questions are factored out to form the results.[485] Hence these measures and the linked questionnaire are developed in all conscience, but there are still some important components relevant for the development of the questionnaire to be discussed. Especially the realisation of pre-test is essential. The literature highlights the importance of this critical evaluation from the outside.[486] Reasons to perform pre-tests are countless. One of the most important reasons is to increase the rate of return due to a better understanding of the questionnaire.[487] Another reason is to prove whether the measures ensure valid and reliable results.[488] This means in other words that a valid measure aims exactly on the area of interest while reliability is a necessary attribute of the data to repeat the survey several times with similar results.[489] This questionnaire was also pre-tested. Several questions were adapted or added during this process a detailed description of this process is part of chapter 7.1.2.

---

[482] See Stier (1999), p.178.
[483] Cf. Tanriverdi/Venkatraman (2005), p.105.
[484] See Schnell et al. (1993), pp.343-344.
[485] See Hübler (2005), p.14.
[486] See Stier (1999), p.184.
[487] See Schnell et al. (1993), pp.358-359.
[488] See Schnell et al. (1993), p.122 and pp.357-359
[489] See Hübler (2005), pp.37-41.

Obviously the perfect data is not available in practice but at least researchers can try to minimise the influence of such imprecise proceeding.[490] Besides this it is important to note that another important formal fact is the language. This questionnaire was developed in German. One of the most vital arguments is that the survey is performed in Germans-speaking countries. Also central is that the used vocabulary is even if strongly adapted still highly specific. Therefore it seems to be the best decision to perform this survey in German in order to support the answering of German-speaking respondents. Further elements, which are important for the development of a questionnaire, are design, format and layout, which are very essential to maximise the attendance in this questionnaire. Thus the questionnaire intends to meet the set standards in reliability, manageability and aesthetics (See Appendix A).[491] Another important reason for this standardised measurement concept in form of a questionnaire provides the opportunity to control the results objectively as the interview process will not be biased through personal interaction of an interviewer.[492] These fundamental rules reflect only partially the rules observed during the phase of designing and formulation.[493] Additionally formal guidelines for questionnaire layout are introduced, all the time, based on standard literature.[494] Trying to achieve these high standards only discreet colours are used in order to highlight important instructions. Besides this several marketing specialists reviewed the questionnaire to achieve the best standard possible. Finally also the realisation of the survey was performed in accordance with the terms defined by the literature. After mailing the questionnaire the first time there was a remembrance phone call after two weeks and a further reminder per mail after one more week.[495] The concrete results and method will be explained in the empirical part in chapter 7. This part is to give a brief overview on the activities which are linked to the design and development of a questionnaire. For complexity reasons and remembering the focus of this book the relatedness measure concept must be in the centre of discussion. Hence the following paragraph will introduce the underlying statistical

---

[490] See Stier (1999), p.51.
[491] See Schnell et al. (1993), pp.370-371.
[492] See Miles/Huberman (1994), p.10.
[493] For more information cf. Schnell et al. (1993), pp.343-373 or Stier (1999), pp.171-184.
[494] Cf. Stier (1999), Hübler (2005) or Schnell et al. (1993).
[495] See Schnell et al. (1993), p.373.

knowledge needed for the development of the measure in chapter 6.2 but also for the empirical analysis in chapter 7.

6.1.3 STATISTICAL BACKGROUND

The statistical dimension is considered for every question which evolves from the operationalisation of the theoretical framework and results in a specific variable. Describing and defining these variables is necessary for several reasons. On the one hand a detailed description of the variables enables other researchers to replicate this study with a new dataset. On the other hand it unfolds possible weaknesses of the data or procedures and opens the analysis to argument.[496] To ease the access to this statistical categories this book gives a brief overview on different variables and their possible characteristics. For a graphical support of the discussed structure see Figure 6-1.

		Identity	Order	Distance	Logical Zero	Information/ Transformation
Qualitative	Nominal (Categorial)	Yes	No	No	No	low high
Quantitative	Ordinal	Yes	Yes	No	No	
	Interval	Yes	Yes	Yes	No	
	Ratio	Yes	Yes	Yes	Yes	high low

Figure 6-1 Overview on Possible Characteristics of Statistical Variables
Source: following Schnell et al. (1993), p.150.

Literature distinguishes three main classifications of variables from different angles. Differentiating **qualitative** and **quantitative** variables is the highest classification and reflects the first angle.[497] Qualitative variables can be specified with regard to a specific characteristic which can not be classified referring to their size and are finite (e.g. nationality of a person or industry of a firm). Alongside the quantitative variables can be differentiated in terms of size.[498] To get a better overview on the different specifications the second level of classification is

---

[496] See Benninghaus (2001), pp.11-12.
[497] See Benninghaus (2001), pp.12-25.
[498] See Klein/Missong (2002), p.8.

introduced where a distinction is drawn between **discrete** and **continuous** variables. It is important to note that qualitative variables are always discrete. By contrast, the continuous measures can reach every value within a given interval (e.g. Revenue of a firm can be measured in billions, millions, thousands, or smaller units in between).[499] The third and last level of classification distinguishes four different forms a variable can take. This scheme defined **nominal** (sometimes known as categorical), **ordinal**, **interval** and **ratio** scales.[500] The information content is increasing from the ordinal to ratio scales, the reasons are discussed afterwards.[501] Beginning with the nominal scale which is fairly simple as it only offers a comparison whether different objects are similar in the dimension tested (e.g. whether firms are acting in the same industry or not). Hence this is a simple scale to classify dimensions but the problems are obvious as no order or further information is given.[502] All other scales include this measure as minimum operational level. The next higher scale is the so called ordinal scale which enables the user to construct orders for the different variable expressions not knowing what the exact distance between these dimensions is (e.g.: Rate the importance of a resource with high or low).[503] Again more information including the operational level of the above scales is delivered by the interval scale. Here the obvious advantage is that a statement about the exact distance between the categories is given but this scale has no absolute zero which means that no information about the ratio between different categories are contained (e.g. the interval between 10° Celsius and 15° Celsius is the same as with 20° and 25°, always five degree Celsius → but you can not say that with 10° Celsius it is half as warm as with 20° Celsius).[504] The ratio scale offers as the name suggests the possibility to get information about the ratio between different values which means that it has an absolute zero or also logical zero. Measures using this scale offer the largest amount of information (e.g. Firm A has revenues 20 billion while Firm B has 10 billion; here it is possible to say that Firm A gains twice as much revenues as Firm B).[505] The last distinction between interval and ratio scale is for most of

---

[499] See Benninghaus (2001), pp.13-14.
[500] See Schnell et al. (1993), p.148.
[501] See Hübler (2005), p.22.
[502] See Bryman/Cramer (1994), p.65.
[503] See Benninghaus (2001), pp.18-19.
[504] See Bryman/Cramer (1994), pp.65-67.
[505] See Stier (1999), p.45.

the analysing tools not relevant. This book will in consequence not make a distinction between interval/ratio.[506] Another important point to note is that a scale with a high level of information (e.g. interval/ratio can be analysed with tools designed for ordinal scales), but at the same time it can only offer information of ordinal scaled information. This process is called transformation. Contrary to the first feeling the ordinal and nominal scaled variables are predominant in econometric empirical analysis and not the highly informative interval/ratio scaled variables.[507] The following analysis is based on this theoretical framework in the same way like the empirical analysis is and is introducing the developed relatedness measure concept.

6.2 MEASURING RELATEDNESS WITH A QUESTIONNAIRE

After a short introduction on the fundamentals of this measure this book is now focusing on the relatedness measure concept. The intention is to give a clear rationale for the chosen structure and questions. For this reason the questionnaire is divided into three sections. Section one is the introduction with two introducing questions, section two are the general questions focusing on the indirect measurement of relatedness while section three and the following sections are concerned about measuring relatedness directly. This will also be the order used below. At this point it is important to note that the theoretical framework and the guidelines discussed before are in the centre of consideration throughout the whole development process. If there are some specific restrictions or theoretical implications they are added in the relevant chapter.

6.2.1 INTRODUCTION AND FRONT PAGE

The intention of the introductory part is to create a "positive climate" for the survey.[508] Hence this part is mainly concerned about an interesting introduction to the relevant topic. The most important element is to ask questions which are easy to answer by almost every addressee.[509] In the beginning this book gives an introduction on the topic and the necessary information on the questionnaire. This

---

[506] See Benninghaus (2001), p.22.
[507] See Hübler (2005), p.23.
[508] See Stier (1999), p.182.
[509] See Schnell et al. (1993), p.371.

is supplemented by the information provided in the cover letter of the e-mail. The intention is to arouse the interest of the reader for this very specific issue. Followed by the first question, which deals with the number of BUs of which a firm consists and how many of these have their own R&D. This question is obviously not very difficult to answer, but nonetheless important for the further analysis of the results. Another important function of this question is to filter out addressees which are not part of the target group even if the first criteria[510] seem to fit into the raster of this study.[511] Hence if a diversified firm does only have one central R&D department they can not provide relevant information for the relatedness of R&D in different BUs. In consequence not answering due to this filter leads to a win-win situation where both parties save time and effort. The operationalisation of this question leads to a quantitative variable with a interval/ratio scale. Hence the information delivered is open to the whole statistical toolbox.[512] Hence this question delivers a very high degree of information.[513] The second question is concerned about the three most important industries which are the main focus of the firm. Even if the question is still easy to answer there are some problems occurring which are always linked to the subjective classification of a firms business to an industry. However, for a possible advanced analysis this industry data might be very important even if the information content is very low as it is a nominal scaled variable which reflects only an identity.[514] Especially if there are some industry specific relatedness phenomena occurring the importance of this variable is increasing. The transition to the following questions is very smooth especially as they are still kept on a very general level but getting more precisely and in consequence more important for the measurement of relatedness in R&D.

6.2.2 CHARACTERISING FIRMS BY ADDITIONAL QUESTIONS

The first two additional questions are different from the other additional questions. They are obviously quantitative and interval/ratio scaled asking for **revenue** and **R&D expenditure** in Euro. Hence these questions deliver a wide range of

---

[510] Cf. selection criteria in chapter 7.1.1.
[511] See Stier (1999), p.183.
[512] Cf. Chapter 5.1.3. and Table 5-1.
[513] See Hübler (2005), p.22.
[514] Cf. Chapter 5.1.3. and Table 5-1.

information that is almost all the time[515] publicly available in annual reports.[516] Especially the revenue and R&D expenditure for the single BU is in the centre of this question; hence the overall revenues and R&D expenditure are by-products which might be relevant for a further testing. Revenue itself is simply a measure of firm or BU size, while R&D expenditure indicates the activity of a firm.[517] The most important reason for these questions as already mentioned is that R&D intensity with respect to sales (cf. chapter 6.2.2.) can easily be calculated. This is one reason for the intensive use of R&D intensities for an indirect measurement of relatedness as described before. Further possible applications of these two variables are the analysis of a firm's success, what does not seem to be necessary in the context of this book. However, this possibility has to be kept in mind as many researchers base their explanation of success on R&D expenditures, at least partially.[518] Besides the standard R&D intensity there is also the possibility to calculate intensity with respect to employees in R&D which gives another possibility for an indirect proxy.[519] This leads to the next important question to be answered which is the **absolute number of employees** and the **number of employees in R&D** in every single BU. Obtaining this detailed information implicitly leads to the data for the whole firm. Employees are a quantitative variable which is interval/ratio scaled. This again means that there is much information provided by this question. Anew the absolute number taken for itself reflects similarly to the revenues the size of a firm.[520] The main intention is again to create some ratios which might help to get a good proxy or some additional information. First there is the ratio which reflects an employment structure and results from the division of the absolute number of employees to the employees in R&D (always for each BU separately).[521] A second ratio could be the number of employees in R&D to the investments made in R&D but as expected they are highly correlated (98%).[522] Therefore a ratio makes obviously no sense. A third measure can be derived from the financial indicators used by the US Federal

---

[515] The availability of the information depends on the underlying accounting standards IFRS, HGB, etc.
[516] See for example Bayer AG (2004), p. 32 (R&D expenditure per BU) and pp.14-22 (segment reporting especially the revenues).
[517] See Fry et al. (2002), p.12.
[518] See Klette/Griliches (2000), pp.363-364.
[519] See Harhoff (1998), p.446.
[520] See Fry et al. (2002), p.12.
[521] See Chiang/Mensah (2004), p.303.
[522] See Harhoff (1998), p.447.

Reserve Bank to judge commercial banks since 1978. Offering information about the revenue generated by each employee.[523] A further interesting measure would be the output of patents per R&D employee or expenditure.[524] This variable is part of the next question. Counting the **number of patents** is as explained in chapter 5.2.2 a often-used proxy to measure indirectly the output of a BU or firm. Thus the importance of this variable is obvious, it can be characterised as a quantitative variable which is based on a interval/ratio scale. As indicated before this measure is not only self-explanatory, it is also very interesting to form some ratios which might help to create a proxy to replicate the resource relatedness indirectly or characterise a firm or a BU in more detail. The problems connected with the patent count are discussed in detail in chapter 5.2. The most common ratio is R&D expenditure per patent.[525] Again the argument alleged before can be applied for the ratio on employees per patent. Another often cited ratio is the so called Patent intensity which is patents divided by total revenue (of a firm or a BU).[526] One more ratio is applied by innovation researchers. This ratio measures the patents per employees or per 1.000 employees dependent on the size of the firm.[527] To give an overview on the discussed variables and some potential ratios see Figure 6-2. Finally there are two last variables which could help to identify relatedness from the outside. As set forth in chapter 3.3, the organisation of R&D is very important for a complete evaluation. Therefore the question for the number of **national and international research sites** should on the one hand help to find the total number of research sites and on the other hand the overview on the degree of internationalisation seems also to be very interesting. It is clear that there are no information about the size of these research sites or the intensity with which research is pushed forward. This discloses the character of the variable which is a interval/ratio scaled quantitative variable and again open to many statistical tools. To complete the indirect measurement of relatedness the final variable is introduced. Asking for the **organisational structure of the R&D departments** within each BU gives in comparison to the other questions only a lower degree of information as this variable is nominal scaled. Hence the answer only helps to form categories as it is a qualitative information about the organisational structure.

---

[523] See Chen (2002), p.202.
[524] See Klette/Griliches (2000), p.370.
[525] See Klette/Griliches (2000), p.370.
[526] See Rogers (2002), p.7.
[527] See Fischer et al. (1994), p.6.

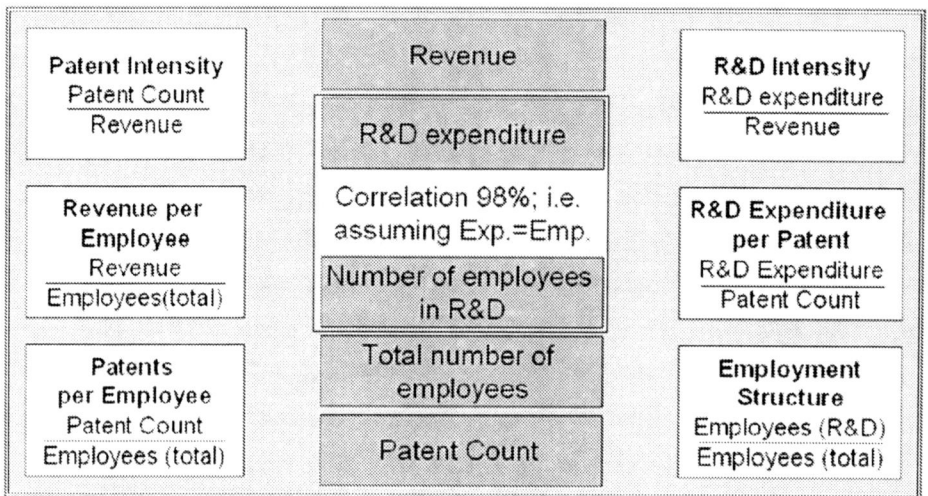

Figure 6-2 Overview on potential indirect measures of relatedness
Source: own Development

6.2.3 SUMMARY OF THE INDIRECT MEASURING CONCEPT OF R&D RELATEDNESS

Figure 6-2 is both, a good overview on variables questioned and a concise summary of potential ratios for measuring relatedness indirectly. This indirect assessable data might serve two objectives for researchers. One objective is to analyse the data derived from the survey in more detail and another objective for future research might be to find a proxy to describe relatedness indirectly as mentioned before. After discussing the indirect assessable data the questions for a direct assessment of relatedness need to be introduced.

6.2.4 MEASURING RELATEDNESS DIRECTLY BY SPECIFIC QUESTIONS

Subsequently to the general questions asked during the first part of the questionnaire, the survey focused on the direct assessment of relatedness of single R&D resources. These questions have been positioned in the last section of the questionnaire and the survey follows the recommendation of STIER. According to this framework, the sensitive and complex questions have to be positioned in later parts of the questionnaire in order to reduce the risk of early abandonment through the respondent.[528] The basis for this approach has been developed in chapter 4.1. The resource base acted as the structural framework for the

---

[528] See Stier (1999), p. 183.

questionnaire. The resources of R&D have been analysed separately to enable a more detailed analysis of relevant resources and relatedness. Therefore every questions of the questionnaire on this area compiles the complete structure of the resource base. The measured resources have been the following:

Tangible resources:
- General infrastructure
- R&D infrastructure
- Expenditures for human resources in R&D

Intangible resources:
- External R&D knowledge
- Internal R&D knowledge
- Mixed/Joint knowledge
- Expertise of R&D personnel (not R&D specific)
- Social/Soft skills of R&D personnel
- Operational structure
- Organisational structure
- External perception of the company (image, brands)
- Internal perception of the company (culture)

Each of the resources is accompanied with precise, however unspecific, examples to give solid guidelines for the respondent. These annexes support the right interpretation of the resource in the question and increase the quality of the questionnaires in general as "wrong" answers will be minimised. A scale is provided to rate each statement from 1 = very high, 2 = high, 3 = average, 4 = low and 5 = very low. Hence, the questionnaire assesses the different dimensions of R&D resources with an ordinal scale.[529] This approach seems necessary, as the respondents might not be able to rate the distinctions between the ratings of different resources appropriately. In consequence, information about the distances of different parameter values is not available directly from this approach.[530] This scale is accompanied with the possibility to reject an answer for each single

---

[529] See Benninghaus (2001), pp.18-19.
[530] See Bryman/Cramer (1994), pp.65-67.

resource. This approach will on the one hand enable respondents to complete the questionnaire if they are not able, not allowed due to communication policy or not willing to rate or answer to specific resources. On the other hand, such evade answers might raise the number as well as the quality of answers.[531] These responses therefore provide an appraisal if a resource can offer joint use through different R&D sites or the transferability of resources respectively.

Figure 6-3 shows the presentation of the resources for the last three sections of the questionnaire. Each question applies a separate dimension across these resources. The questionnaire assesses therefore not only the single dimension of measuring relatedness. Moreover, questions on the synergies arising from this relatedness and on the relevance of single resources are included. This approach seems to be necessary to give an entire and well-structured view on the resource base relevant for R&D units. This approach enables the analysis of resources and the combination of different point of views on the same subject matter.

---

[531] See Stier (1999), p. 183.

Ressourcen	sehr hoch 1	hoch 2	durch- schnittlich 3	gering 4	sehr gering 5	k.A.
Bereich der materiellen Ressourcen						
Allg. materielle Ressourcen (wie z.B. IT-Netzwerke, Arbeitsplatzausstattung u.a.)	☐	☐	☐	☐	☐	☐
F&E spezifische Ressourcen (wie z.B. Labortechnik/- ausstattung, u.a.)	☐	☐	☐	☐	☐	☐
Absolute Personalausstattung im Bereich F&E (als reine quantitative Angabe)	☐	☐	☐	☐	☐	☐
Bereich der immateriellen Ressourcen						
Externes technologiebasiertes (F&E-spezifisches) Wissen (wie z.B. Lizenzen, u.ä. Ressourcen)	☐	☐	☐	☐	☐	☐
Internes technologiebasiertes (F&E-spezifisches) Wissen (wie z.B. Patente, u.ä. aus Grundlagenforschung, angewandte Forschung und Entwicklung)	☐	☐	☐	☐	☐	☐
(F&E-spezifisches) Mischwissen (z.B. aus Kooperationen mit Unternehmen, Universitäten etc.)	☐	☐	☐	☐	☐	☐
Fachwissen der Mitarbeiter, das nicht F&E-spezifisch ist (wie z.B. Prozesswissen, Produktionswissen etc.)	☐	☐	☐	☐	☐	☐
Soziale Kompetenz (Soft Skills) der Mitarbeiter (wie z.B. Kommunikations- und Konfliktlösungstechniken etc.)	☐	☐	☐	☐	☐	☐
Ablaufstruktur im Rahmen der Unternehmensstruktur (wie z.B. Gremien, Workflows oder Datenmanagement etc.)	☐	☐	☐	☐	☐	☐
Aufbaustruktur im Rahmen der Unternehmensstruktur (wie z.B. hierarchische Organisation oder Informationsdurchlässigkeit, Bürokratie etc.)	☐	☐	☐	☐	☐	☐
Externe Wahrnehmung des Unternehmens (durch z.B. Image, Marken u.ä.)	☐	☐	☐	☐	☐	☐
Interne Wahrnehmung des Unternehmens (durch z.B. Kultur, Innovationsfreude, Selbsteinschätzung etc.)	☐	☐	☐	☐	☐	☐
	1 sehr hoch	2 hoch	3 durch- schnittlich	4 gering	5 sehr gering	k.A.

Figure 6-3 Resources within the questionnaire

Source: own development

6.2.4.1 CROSS-FUNCTIONAL USABILITY

In the final part of this questionnaire the first question tries to measure, if resources in R&D can be used across different BUs. The respondents were asked to state the ability of each single resource to be applied in different R&D units. The previously described five-digit scale has been provided for answering. With this approach, the book follows the argumentation presented by the most recent empirical papers on resource relatedness.[532] This question aims at contributing an insight into the actual and individual rating of the usage of single resources. This dimension of resource analysis seems to be from major importance. Results from

---

[532] See Tanriverdi (2006), Tanriverdi (2005) and Tanriverdi/Venkatraman (2005).

this question enable first insights into the nature of single resources. This approach therefore measures relatedness of single resources and provides as well basic information for the analysis of the following questions. The measurement of relatedness of R&D is the major objective of this book. Using this questionnaire and the information of this question, relatedness can be measured directly on firm level.[533] Information about relatedness can be extracted directly from the answers of this question and can be analysed with simple descriptive empirical methods. Hence, the main task of this book can be fulfilled directly with this approach. However, as this book is going to investigate the relationship between relatedness and success of R&D, further information about the underlying resources for R&D have to be accessed.

6.2.4.2 POTENTIAL SYNERGIES BASED ON RELATED RESOURCES

Based on the results of the previous question, the questionnaire asks for the potential synergies arising from related resources. By this query, this book tries to find arguments for the well-known statement that synergies arise from related resource. This approach is founded on the very basics of the RBV and can be found across all major papers provided e.g. by FARJOUN,[534] MARKIDES and WILLIAMSON[535] or ROBINS and WIERSEMA.[536] However, as TANRIVERDI and VENKATRAMAN stress, not every resource offers the same synergy potential.[537] Different resources can be related across different BUs but offer just low synergies. This might result from arising dissynergies or through missing possibilities to generate synergies through economies of scope or other effects.[538] Especially resources in R&D might be affected as the dominance of intangible resources in R&D offer a wide range of potential dissynergies e.g. through the tacitness of knowledge.[539] Hence, it seems useful to include this question in order to analyse the actual synergy potential arising from relatedness. In addition, results from this question might act as a crosscheck for the basic assumptions of

---

[533] The book therefore measures relatedness according to the recommendation of Tanriverdi and Venkatraman. See Tanriverdi/Venkatraman (2005), p. 98.
[534] See Farjoun (1994), p. 196.
[535] See Markides/Williamson (1996), p. 340.
[536] See Robins/Wiersema (1995), p. 277.
[537] See Tanriverdi/Venkatraman (2005), p. 100.
[538] See the discussion of synergies and dissynergies in chapter 4.
[539] See Tanriverdi/Venkatraman (2005), p. 100.

the RBV. The respondents will be given the same ranking order, previously described (five digit scale) and will be asked to estimate the synergies from related resources based on their point of view. Hence, this question enables the possibility to analyse the relationship between relatedness and synergies directly. The results will offer information about the different synergy contribution of different resources.

6.2.4.3 RELEVANCE OF SINGLE RESOURCES FOR THE R&D PROCESS

The last section of the questionnaire addresses the relevance of single resources for the R&D process. This question seems necessary to gain detailed information about the resource base within R&D. This book applies the RBV on R&D units only. In contrast to most of the literature, which focuses either on diversification in general or on single resources,[540] relatedness is going to be analysed on the whole resource base applicable for R&D. Therefore the relation between single resources has to be addressed in order to achieve a complete picture of resources in R&D.

To give empirical support to this approach, the questionnaire includes the request to rate the contribution of single resources to the success of the R&D process. During a first step, the respondents were asked to give their statement for every single resource and its contribution to R&D success. There the respondents found, once again, the same five digit scaling to rate their statement. These answers will give a detailed insight into the relevance of single resources. During a second step, the informants were asked to bring all twelve resources into one ranking, starting with the most relevant counting on to the least relevant. This additional request to respondents has been included to overcome the lack of information of the used ordinal scale. The ranking will offer supplementary information on this dimension, as these are necessary for a reasonable interpretation of the relevance of single resources. This request will on the one hand act as a crosscheck for the previous given answers and on the other hand will offer a relative order within the resource base of R&D. The measurement of relevance of single resources should be included in the discussion on R&D resources as related resources and synergies from related resources do not assess the importance of single resources

---

[540] See e.g. Markides/Williamson (1996) or Tanriverdi (2006).

within the R&D process. Different resources contribute differently to the success of R&D projects. Therefore this book has to include a dimension of relevance within the analysis of resources to give a detailed view on the impact of resource relatedness.

6.2.4.4 EMPIRICAL HYPOTHESES BASED ON THE MEASUREMENT CONCEPT

Based on the concept of the three dimensions on resource relatedness, the resource base of R&D can be outlined in an all-embracing way. The questionnaire approach enables this book to highlight the interdependencies between single resources through the assessment of the factors relatedness, synergies and relevance for success. In contrast to the relative straight evaluation of the answers on single questions, the measurement of relations between these dimensions will require more complex statistical instruments.[541] Based on this concept, the empirical approach will be based on the following hypothesises.

The RBV stresses the relationship between relatedness and synergy. Related resources are the main source for synergies arising through the diversification of corporations.[542] This should be applicable for resources within R&D as structured by CHATTERJEE and WERNERFELT.[543] Hence, the first hypothesis developed within this approach will be:

H1:   *Within the resource base of R&D of diversified corporations, increasing resource relatedness will foster the occurrence of potential synergies.*

Following the RBV will lead to the acknowledgement of the relevance of synergies for the overall success of diversification.[544] In the environment of diversified companies, the generation of synergies contribute meaningfully to the benefits arising from cooperation between different BUs.[545] Applying this approach to R&D departments, synergies from joint use and transfer of resources will contribute to the success of the overall R&D success. Hence, these synergies are of striking

---

[541] See chapter 7.
[542] See Markides/Williamson (1996), p. 340, Tanriverdi (2006), p. 62 or others.
[543] See Chatterjee/Wernerfelt (1991).
[544] See the arguments presented by Prahalad/Hamel (1990), p. 81.
[545] See Tanriverdi (2006), p. 57.

relevance for the accomplishment of R&D projects.[546] Thus, these assumptions will lead to the following second hypothesis:

H2-1: *Resources with high potential synergies will be rated with a higher relevance for the R&D process than resources with low potential synergies.*[547]

Another point of view, generally stated in the context of resources in R&D is the importance of intangible resources.[548] In addition, intangible resources offer a higher chance of cross-functional usage through the transfer of these resources in contrast to the joint use of tangible resources. This had been shown during the development of the relevant resource base of R&D in the earlier part of this book.[549] R&D processes rely to a high degree on the exploration of existing knowledge in order to generate additional knowledge.[550] Hence this book will include the empirical verification of this point of view. This can be expressed with the following third hypothesis.

H2-2: *In R&D, knowledge based resources might be counted as the most relevant resources. The kind of resources contributes meaningfully to the relevance of this resource for the overall success of the R&D process.*

Obviously, the different arguments presented in case for H2-1 and H2-2 might be conflictive to a certain degree. Hence the valuation of these different perspectives will be one of the tasks of the empirical investigation in order to highlight the relevance of different resources. Following this research question and in combination with the first hypothesis, this empirical approach will contribute a wholesale outline of the resources in R&D referencing the RBV.

---

[546] See Tanriverdi/Venkatraman (2005), p. 97.
[547] The occurrence of synergies from resource relatedness will lead to an increasing relevance of related resources for the overall success of the R&D process. Thus, increasing synergy potential of related resources will lead to an improved rating of the relevance of these resources for the R&D process.
[548] See Del Canto/Gonzalez, (1999), p. 897.
[549] See the arguments presented during the development of the resource base in chapter 4.1.
[550] See Lynskey (1999), p. 317.

6.2.4.5 SUMMARY OF THE MEASUREMENT CONCEPT OF R&D RELATEDNESS

Summarised, the questionnaire compiles three different dimensions on the assessment of R&D resources and their relatedness. Relevant information from this questionnaire will be about relatedness of single resources. This output is the key objective of this book. However, additional information about resources will be generated through questions about the context of resources in R&D. Following this approach will contribute to the quality of the empirical method. Not only the "pure" relatedness will be assessed, but also the quality of this relatedness. In consequence the quality of this empirical framework will increase significantly. Through the measurement of synergies arising from relatedness this empirical appraisal will offer deeper information about the basic assumptions of the RBV and a more detailed knowledge about the characteristics of resources in R&D. The third dimension "relevance of resources" offers the possibility to class R&D resources according to their total relevance for the R&D process. In this context, information might be accessed about the theoretical relevance of synergies and actual relevance of resources. Hence, this questionnaire offers an exhaustive approach for the research on resource relatedness in R&D.

7 EMPIRICAL ANALYSIS

After introducing the survey concept of this book in detail it is now necessary to formulate the basic assumptions and conditions of the data ascertainment. In this context basic analysis of the sample and responses and the connected response rate and finally the information competency are assessed. The second part of this chapter comprises a univariate and a multivariate analysis. The univariate analysis is used to explain the sample and identify especially the relatedness of resources. Finally the multivariate analysis is used in order to analyse the hypotheses introduced in chapter 6.2.4.

7.1 DATA

At the beginning of this paragraph it is necessary to note that the basic principles for the development of a theoretical framework and a questionnaire (cf. chapter 6.1) are applied all the time. These and the following principles of data ascertainment are necessary to achieve the highest degree of validity[551] and reliability possible.[552] First the sample is examined and explained, the second area to be treated is the administration concerned to raise the return rate with a good questionnaire and after treatment of the addresses to increase the response rate. This response rate will be discussed in the final paragraph of this chapter strongly linked to the information competency which is also assessed.

7.1.1 SAMPLE

The sample for this study contained MBFs with **at least two BUs**. For this reason the firm data of OSIRIS[553] was analysed in the following indices: DAX 30, MDAX, SDAX (DAX 120), TECDAX, ATX Prime and SMI. These indices are composed of a large fraction of conglomerate diversified firms. Another reason for extending the German Prime Standard by the ATX Prime and SMI was the awareness of the possibility of a low rate of return and a high failure quota which is often linked to so

---

[551] For more information on validity and reliability cf. chapter 5.1.2. or Stier (1999), pp.51-62.
[552] See Stier (1999), pp.51-62.
[553] See Osiris (2006).

called "mail surveys".[554] Besides the two BUs another criterion was that **no pure trade, service or financial firms** were addressed. This decision was based on an interview with the head of research from a large financial service provider who stated that they do perform research (mathematical, statistical modelling etc.) but not in the sense of this book (cf. chapter 3.2).[555] In consequence the decision was clear and the number of firms was reduced from 221 to 157 (see Table 7-1). One firm was added to the sample, as this family owned firm had special interest in the research of this book and in consequence supported this research. Finally the sample counts 158 firms which fulfilled the criteria discussed before. The addresses were dependent on the information available either head of corporate communication or senior R&D executives, the actual informant competency will be in the centre of the following paragraph. At this point it is important to keep in mind that direct and indirect data is ascertained by this survey.[556] So the addressees need a very good overview on the R&D activities themselves but also on the whole firm with all its BUs. The following paragraph is specifically dealing with the activities concerned about deriving a good response rate, but also with the informant competency.

7.1.2 ADMINISTRATION, RESPONSE RATES AND INFORMANT COMPETENCY

The **administration** is following the theoretical approaches described in the relevant literature. Especially the pre-tests which were performed beforehand are an important detail. This questionnaire was tested by ten persons concerned with questionnaires and their development, but also with practitioners who are engaged in R&D or at least have a good overview on R&D in their firm. The time for each pre-test averaged out at 40 minutes. Literature highlights the importance of this critical evaluation from outside.[557] The pre-test especially assessed the face and the content of the questionnaire to indemnify a high validity of the survey.[558]

---

[554] See Stier (1999), p.198.
[555] According to a pre-test interview with the head of research of one of the major international insurance firms, the research conducted by financial service providers is mainly connected with financial or economic research and hence not comparable with the research described by the OECD (1992). Additional, the described research units merely act as a background information supplier for other corporate areas. Based on this interview, firms have been excluded from the sample when they do not perform research in the traditionally sense of the OECD.
[556] See Stier (1999), p.198.
[557] See Stier (1999), p.184, cf. also chapter 6.1.
[558] See Schnell et al. (1993), pp.356-359.

Another form of pre-test was performed with the documents containing the questionnaire to ensure that the document is fully functional in every possible combination of operating systems. Similar procedures of testing were applied on the word document which was equipped with programmed answer fields to relieve the addresses while answering the questionnaire at the computer. To reduce the risk of failure the original Word document was supplemented by a PDF. Another reason to attach a PDF was that many people like reading from papers. In consequence addresses had two possibilities two return their questionnaire either by e-mail or by fax. These arrangements lead to an error ratio that is with 1 out of 158 firms very low. This firm had a software incompatibility problem so that the questionnaire was unreadable.

Despite the preparation discussed before, the **response rate** underperformed the expectations. A detailed view on the response rate is in the centre of the following depiction. The questionnaire was sent to 158 firms. After the first two weeks the first dead line passed and only four firms (2.7%) had replied and 21 (14.2%) firms rejected participation formally by mail. After starting to follow up the addressees by phone calls (one time) and by mail (three times) the response rate increased but nonetheless remained very low. The deadline was postponed during this process for three more weeks on an overall of five weeks. This procedure is largely following the approaches on mail surveys described in literature.[559] One of the answered questionnaires had to be deleted as a firm answered it twice, one time from a divisional point of view and the second time from the headquarters point of view which was finally used. The rejections increased especially based on the phone calls by 26 on an overall of 45 (28.7%). Hence the overall rate of response stayed as already explained very low at 10 (6.4%) answered questionnaires adding one questionnaire from a privately owned firm which ends in 11 (7%) answered questionnaires. Explaining these low response rates seems to be difficult, a few suggestions however are very self-evident. One influence was the football world cup which was interacting with the summer time which caused low personal availability and in consequence weak answering capabilities in at least 20% of the rejections. One more reason to be added is resulting from the reverse of the answering addresses who were all highly qualified managers; many firms

---

[559] See Schnell et al. (1993), p.372.

are not willing or able to give a questionnaire to highly qualified managers. To get a better overview on the structure of responding and non-responding firms table 7-1 is highlighting the most important facts.

Countries&Indices / Relevant Figures	Germany S-DAX, M-DAX, DAX 30 and TecDAX	Switzerland SMI	Austria ATX	Sum
Firms overall	148	28	45	221
Sample*	116	10	31	157 + (1)
Rejections	32	4	9	45
Rejection Rate	27.6%	40.0%	29.0%	28.7% (28.5%)
Responses	6	1	3	10 + (1)
Response Rate	4.1%	3.6%	6.7%	6.3% (7.0%)
No Response	78	5	19	102
No Response Rate	67.2%	50.0%	61.3%	65.0% (64.6%)

* The sample was chosen with regard to the two criteria developed before: 1. Firms with at least two business units and 2. Firms which are not only involved in trade, services and/or financial services. The allocation of the sample over the different countries expressed as a ratio of Sample/Sum of Samples is as follows: Germany: 74%; Switzerland: 6% and Austria: 20%. Also important to note is that the single family owned firm is not part of this analysis.

Table 7-1 Overview on the Sample and Respondent Structure
Source: Own Survey

After discussing the response rate the **informant competency** needs to be highlighted in order to proof that the answered questionnaires are answered by qualified persons. Four questionnaires (36%) were answered by executive employees or directors with a managerial background but still with a focus and overview on R&D. Two of these executive employees were managers of R&D within their firm. Seven (64%) questionnaires were answered by senior executives or by directors/heads of R&D departments.

7.1.3 VALIDATION

Prior to the data analysis there is a high relevance of validating the received data in order to increase the validity of this empirical part. For this reason the received questionnaires were analysed and completed if possible. Hence questions with data publicly available via the Internet or other sources were proved to be consistent. A further intervention to increase the validity of the data was the completion of questions which were not completely answered. These arrangements were only in parts possible for the first part of the questionnaire from question 1 to 9 in different depth. While revenue data is very easy accessible also for single BUs, patent data is usually not available for single BUs depending on the organisational structure of a firm. In this context it is important to note that no data within the questionnaire was changed, only supplemented.

Summarising this chapter shows that despite the administration following the literature on empirical studies the response rate was lower than the response rate of comparable surveys with almost 40% of responding addresses.[560] Nonetheless the informant competency is very high and might in combination with the validated data lead to some useful and interesting results of the empirical analysis performed in the next paragraph.

7.2   DESCRIPTIVE ANALYSIS OF THE DATA

The descriptive analysis of the available data will be the first important step on the way to measuring relatedness and also to get an overview on the data collected. Therefore the first part of this analysis is focusing on the univariate analysis which will be followed by a multivariate analysis in the second part of this chapter. This chapter is obviously very important as it is testing whether the design of the measures and the operation works out and leads to some helpful results for resource relatedness in R&D.

7.2.1   UNIVARIATE DATA ANALYSIS

Important to keep in mind for the following analysis is that not all questions were answered completely by all respondents which leads to changing sample sizes in-between different questions. The univariate analysis itself is divided into two sections. First, the introductory and general part is analysed with its questions from one to nine. In the second part the super ordinate target of measuring resource relatedness in R&D is addressed. Further objectives in this part are the

---

[560] Cf. Tanriverd (2005), pp.321-322.

description of the potential synergies and the success of R&D for each of the single resources.

7.2.1.1 ANALYSIS OF THE INTRODUCTORY PART AND GENERAL DATA AVAILABLE

Beginning this analysis with some basic information on the firms that answered the questionnaire is helpful to assess the available data. All firms which answered the questionnaire had at least two **BUs**; the average firm of this survey has 4.5 BUs. The maximum number of BUs was 14 which reflect 9% of the firms. In contrast to this lonely maximum the minimum of two BUs was stated by 36.4% of the firms. Asking for the **BUs performing R&D** brought an average of 3.9 BUs that perform R&D. Meaning that not all BUs perform R&D. The maximum number of BUs concerned with R&D was thirteen which reflects again 9% of the answers which is similar to the minimum of one BU (cf. Figure 7-1).

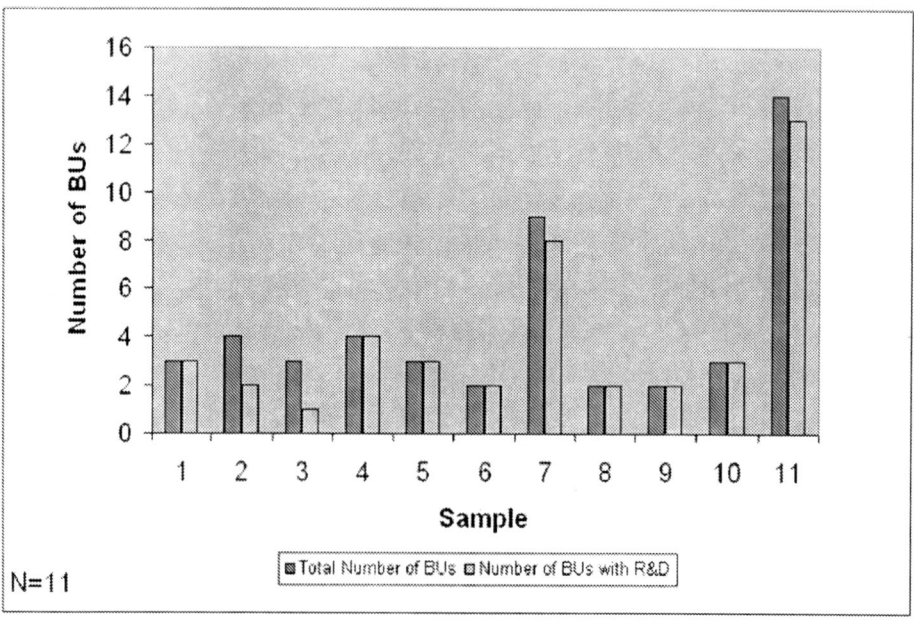

Figure 7-1 Overview on the total number of BUs and BUs with R&D
Source: own Survey

The next question was asking for the **most important industries** served by the firms. In this case the majority of 73% is primarily focusing on the industrial sector.

While 18% focus primarily on the pharmaceutical or chemical industry and 9% are focusing on IT or Telecommunication. Considering the second most important industry showed that 73% of the firms are highly focused and do not serve another industry. Nonetheless 18% are serving miscellaneous industries not identified in detail while 9% serve the IT or Telecommunication industry. None of the firms stated to have a third important industry in their portfolio. Figure 7-2 reflects the answering structure for this question.

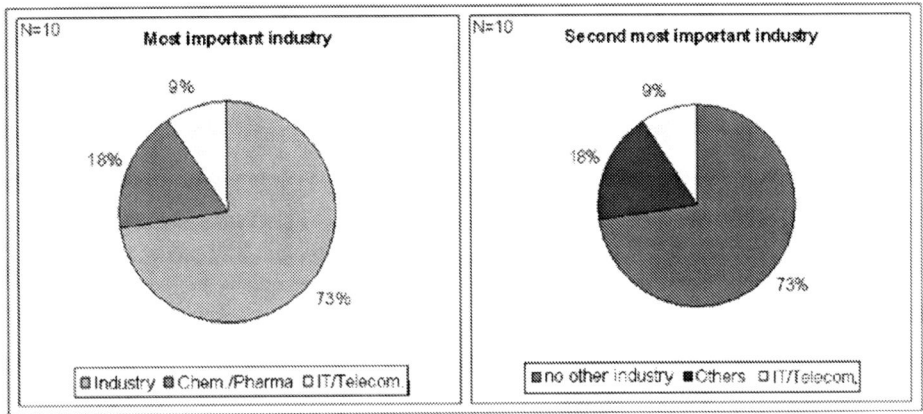

Figure 7-2 The most important and the second most important industry
Source: own Survey

After describing the introductory part of the survey the following part will focus on the more specific but still general questions on the firm and its inputs, outputs and some structures. The first important figure to be discussed is the **revenue** of the answering firms. This figure is very difficult to interpret as the minimum (57 MEUR) and the maximum (7,200 MEUR) are very widespread which leads to an average revenue of 2,169 MEUR. Focusing on the revenues of the BUs points out that this area seems to be more sensitive as the data is offered more restrictive. Only 73% gave detailed information on their revenues within the BUs. Nonetheless 91% can be analysed due to official available annual reports. For a better understanding it seems to be helpful to give a short graphical overview on the allocation of the revenues (cf. Figure 7.3). The revenues will also help to sort and analyse the expenditures in R&D relatively. Especially as the absolute values do not help if the firms are so different in size and structure like these firms are.

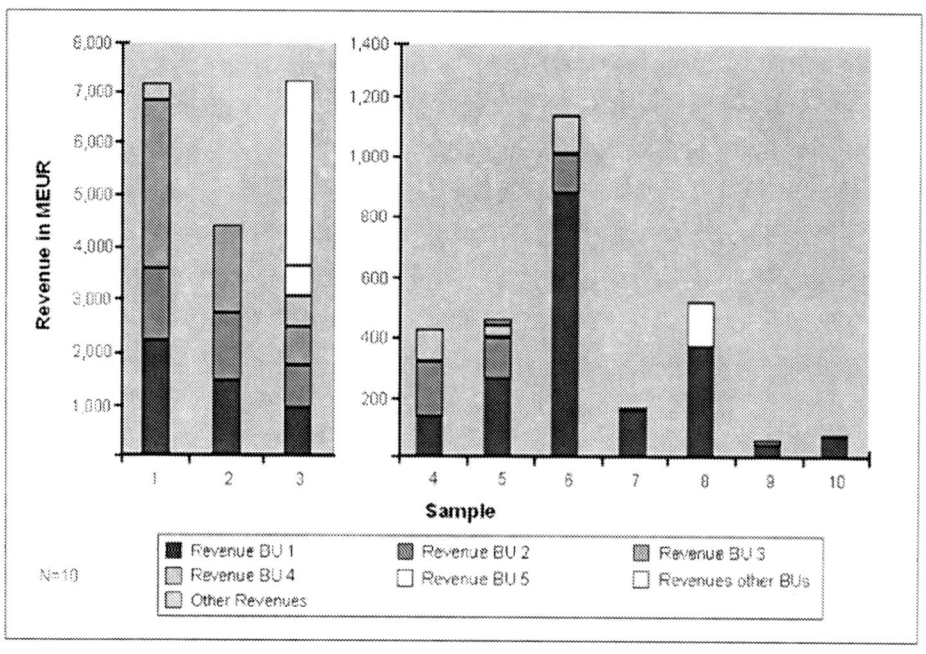

Figure 7-3 Overview on structure and total amount of revenues

Source: own Survey

After describing the revenues this analysis is focusing on the **personnel** gaining these revenues. The data for the absolute headcount was completely available. The minimum is an overall of 280 employees while the maximum is 18,000. This again shows that there is very wide spread. Hence the mean of 5,892 again is of restricted explanatory power. As introduced before the data is graphically displayed in Figure 7-4 to alleviate the absorption of the available information. As the data is varying widely the EMPLOYMENT STRUCTURE introduced in chapter 6.2.2 might help to analyse the results of the survey. The ratio varies also from zero percent up to 25.9%. Summarising the results of the ratio, there might be three groups identified: first the firms with a ratio larger than zero but smaller than ten. A second group which employs ten percent up to 19.99% of their overall employees in R&D while a third group can be characterised by a ratio larger than 20%. The expenditures caused by these employees and other R&D specific expenditures are analysed in the following paragraph.

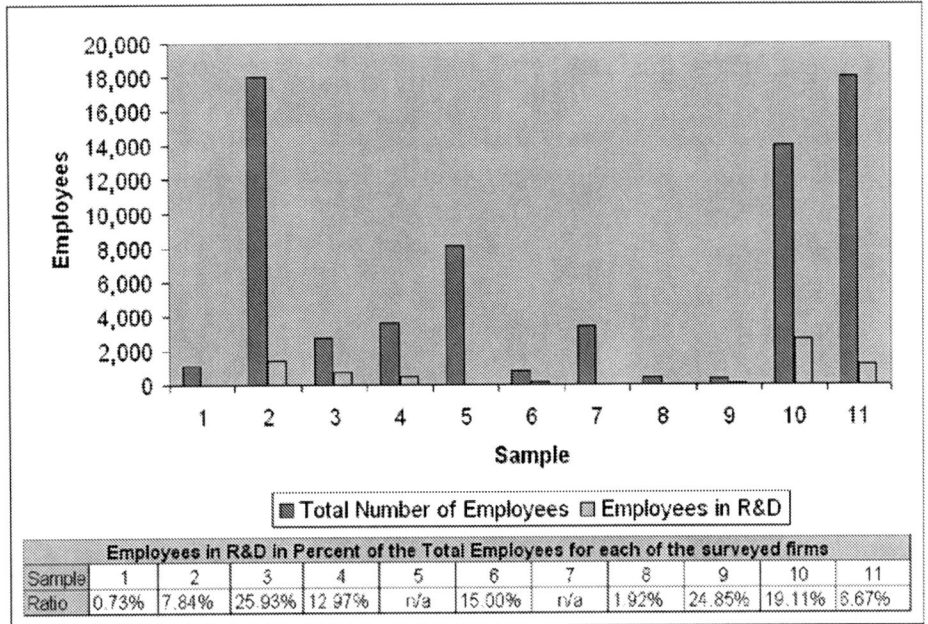

Employees in R&D in Percent of the Total Employees for each of the surveyed firms

Sample	1	2	3	4	5	6	7	8	9	10	11
Ratio	0.73%	7.84%	25.93%	12.97%	n/a	15.00%	n/a	1.92%	24.85%	19.11%	6.67%

Figure 7-4 Overview on the employment structure

Source: own Survey

Discussing the **expenditures in R&D** seems to be a very sensitive area as only 46% answered this question completely. By adding external available data this rate could be increased by 18% on 64%. In contrast to the minimum expenditure which amounts at 1.5 MEUR the maximum amounts at 194 MEUR the mean is situated at 41.7 MEUR. In order to get a better overview on the expenditures the analysis is performed relatively to the revenues of the firm with the so called R&D intensity (cf. chapter 6.2.2). The result shows that there are again three groups that can be determined. First there is a large group of five firms that spend more than zero but less than three percent of their revenues in R&D. A second group of two firms is spending more than three but less than nine percent while the last group consists of two firms that spend more than nine percent of their revenues in R&D. Comparing these figures with international standards is almost impossible as these intensities are diverging from sector to sector. Nonetheless the surveyed firms reflect with 4.22 percent R&D intensity an international average of four in Japan and four and a half percent in the US very well.[561] Further details on

---

[561] See DTI (2005), p.5.

expenditures in R&D especially the data for the single BUs are contained in Figure 7-5.

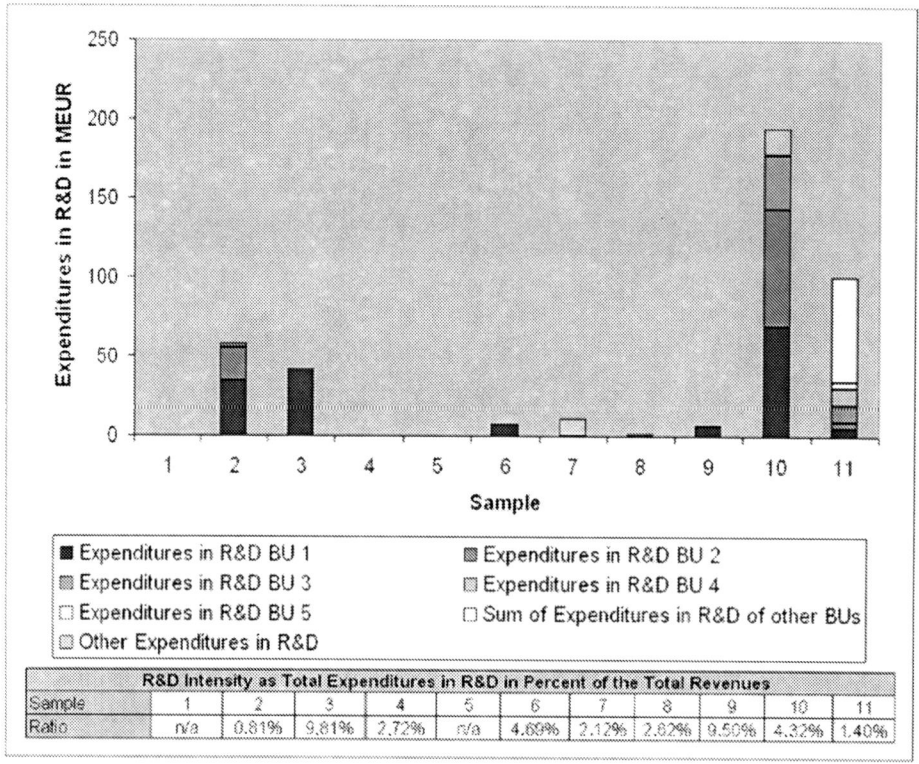

R&D Intensity as Total Expenditures in R&D in Percent of the Total Revenues										
Sample	1	2	3	4	5	6	7	8	9	10	11
Ratio	n/a	0.81%	9.81%	2.72%	n/a	4.69%	2.12%	2.62%	9.50%	4.32%	1.40%

Figure 7-5 Overview on the expenditures in R&D

Source: own Survey

Reaching another sensitive question which is dealing with the **patents** pended over the last two years 2004 and 2005. This question was only answered by 54% of the respondents completely while 46% hesitated to answer. Hence almost half of the respondents denied disclosing their patent count. Investigating patent data for a firm is not that difficult as the data is online available from the "Deutsches Patent- und Markenamt".[562] In consequence the overall patent count for every firm is complete for the last two years (2004 and 2005). Analysing the given data the average patent output per firm over two years is 31 patents. The minimum output

---

[562] In this case it is not necessary to investigate further patent data from other countries as these patents are usually protecting the same invention as in other countries. Hence the patent count would be artificially increased without giving more information about the actual output of a firm. Also important is to note that the number of patents does not say anything about the quality. For more information see Grindley/Teece (1997).

in patents is zero while the maximum output is 220. In consequence a patent count seems not to be very reliable for an objective relatedness measure.

The geographical and structural organisation of R&D are the last questions to be analysed within this general part. First the **geographical structure** of R&D or in other words the number of national and international research sites is described. Almost all firms answered this question (91%) and examining the national research centres the minimum is one national research site while the maximum is seven national research sites. The average firm has 3.2 national research sites. Interesting is the inspection of the international research sites which has a lower minimum of zero but also a higher maximum of 21. This results in a higher average of 3.7 international research sites for the firms polled in this survey. This would lead to the suggestion that there is a tendency of internationalisation but there is another important result that only 60% of the ten answering firms own international research sites. In other words firms that are internationally active push these activities much more than their national activities. Nonetheless there is an overall number of national and international research sites of 69 which leads to an average of 6.9 research sites per firm. Alongside the **organisational structure** is prompted. The result is that all firms answered this question so the data for 43 BUs in 11 firms is available. Suggesting that two dominant organisational forms exist which is on the one hand the centralised organisation which is implemented by 15 BUs (35%). On the other hand there is the decentralised organisation implemented by 22 BUs (51%). Nonetheless the two other organisational forms centralised with competence centre and decentralised with competence centre are implemented with 2 (5%) and 4 (9%) BUs. After this basic overview on the sample the three dimensions are analysed univariately.

7.2.1.2 ANALYSIS OF THE DATA AVAILABLE ON THREE DIMENSIONS

The first dimension to be focused on with an univariate analysis in this chapter is the **measuring of relatedness** between the single resources. This question – as introduced before – is based on possible answers from 1-very high relatedness to 5-very low relatedness. To present a complete picture each, of the resources observed is presented separately. This process is strictly linked to the order developed before (cf. chapter 4.1.2) which is also used in the questionnaire. In consequence the first type of resources is tangible resources. The resource to be measured is the *general infrastructure*. This resource was one of three highly valued resources with a mean value of two on the scale. That means that the general infrastructure is highly related between different BUs performing R&D. The minimum value specified is the one while the maximum value is the three. The second tangible resource analysed is the *R&D infrastructure* with a mean of 2.45 this resource is not as highly related as the general infrastructure. Focusing on the minima and maxima it occurs that the minimum is a one while the maximum value for the R&D infrastructure is five. The last tangible resource is the importance of personnel headcount in R&D. This resource was similarly valued like the specific R&D resources with a mean of 2.5; a minimum of one and maximum of five. Hence the relatedness between the different BUs in the functional area of R&D seems to be high in the area of tangible resources. The following resources are of intangible nature. First there is the *external R&D knowledge* with a mean of three. Hence the relatedness of external R&D knowledge is only of average degree. The minimum is one more time one while the maximum is five. The second intangible resource is the *internal R&D knowledge* which intuitively seems to be a related resource. Support is provided by the results of the survey with a mean of 2 it can be suggested that this resource can be characterised with a high relatedness. The minimum for internal R&D knowledge is one and the maximum is three which is again a very strong sign for the importance of this resource. The third intangible resource to be discussed is *mixed/joint knowledge* which is with a mean of 2.8 obviously not as related as the internal knowledge. Hence it does not surprise that the minimum is one and the maximum is five which reflects the whole range of possible relatedness. The fourth resource is the *expertise of R&D personnel* which is not R&D specific. In this case the mean suggests a mean relatedness of 2.36 with a minimum of two and a maximum of four. This leads to the suggestion that this resource is of higher relatedness than the average of the resources but nonetheless not as high as the two, up to now, most related resources (General Equipment and Internal R&D Knowledge). Followed by an intangible resource with a weaker relatedness of 2.89 the *soft skills of R&D personnel*. In comparison to the other resources observed this is the second worst degree of relatedness with a maximum of one and a minimum of four. The sixth intangible resource is the *operational structure* which is according to the results one of the three highly related resources with a mean of 2.0. The minimum is one and the maximum is three which supports the suggestion that this resource is very related in almost every firm. After discussing the operational structure the organisational structure is in the centre of discussion with a mean of 2.72 the relatedness is not as high as with other resources already analysed. This is supported by the minimum of 1 and the maximum of five which again reflects the whole range of answers. The last but one resource prompted is the *external perception of the company* (image, brands) and its relatedness. Again the relatedness is intuitively suggested to be high and the results support this intuition. With a mean of 2.3 and extreme values of one (minimum) and four (maximum) the external perception seems to be part of the resources with a high relatedness. Finally the internal perception of the company (culture) is the last resource measured. In this case the mean is 2.8 which indicates that this resource is not as related as other resources discussed before. This finding is supported by a minimum of two and a maximum of five what indicates a weaker relationship between the internal perceptions of different BUs than observed with other resources. An overview on the relatedness on the results discussed before is displayed in table 7-2.

	Resource Relatedness in R&D	Observations	Mean	Standard Deviation	Min	Max
1	General infrastructure	11	2.00	0.77	1	3
2	R&D infrastructure	11	2.45	1.04	1	5
3	R&D personnel (headcount)	10	2.50	1.08	1	5
4	External R&D knowledge	11	3.00	1.18	1	5
5	Internal R&D knowledge	11	2.00	0.63	1	3
6	Mixed/Joint knowledge	10	2.80	1.32	1	5
7	Expertise of R&D personnel (not R&D specific)	11	2.36	0.67	2	4
8	Social/Soft skills of R&D personnel	9	2.89	1.05	1	4
9	Operational structure	11	2.00	0.45	1	3
10	Organisational structure	11	2.73	1.10	1	5
11	External perception	10	2.30	0.82	1	4
12	Internal perception	10	2.80	1.14	2	5

Table 7-2 Resource relatedness in R&D

Source: own Survey

Summarising the results of measuring resource based relatedness leads to the suggestions that there are on the one hand several resources (1, 5 and 9) that suggest to be more related than other resources. On the other hand there are resources (4, 6, 8 and 12) which might be in comparison to the three resources mentioned before not as highly related. Nonetheless this ranking does not give any information about the absolute degree of relatedness or the distance between the different resources as this result only offers an order. Hence no information about the distance between these resources is delivered.

The next question is concerned about the same resources in R&D but this time in the context of **potential synergies** arising with these specific resources. At the beginning a short remark on the number of observations received. With an average number of observations of almost 9 there were almost with every resource respondents who did not answer the question. Reasons for this result a manifold but one possible source for this result is the use of the expression "synergies" which is a very abstract expression. Nonetheless the results are interesting and subject to the following discussion. The order of the resources is maintained like before. Therefore the first three resources are tangibles while the rest is intangible. Firstly the *general infrastructure* is analysed and with a mean of two it is given a high potential of synergies. The minimum is one while the maximum is three. Secondly *R&D infrastructure* with a mean of 1.8 is given an even higher potential for synergies with a similar minimum and maximum as before. The third and last tangible resource is the *R&D personnel* which is rated with a mean of 2.20 for its potential synergies. The minimum is again one while the maximum for R&D personnel is four. Hence this resource is out of the tangible resources the one with the least synergy potential even if it is still high. After examining tangible resources the nine intangible resources are in the centre of evaluation. *External R&D knowledge* with a mean of 2.56 is at least not seen as likely as the tangible resources for arising synergies. The minimum and maximum is similar to the resource before (1 and 4). In opposition to the external R&D knowledge stands the *internal R&D knowledge* which is rated with a mean of 2.11 with a higher potential synergy. This is also reflected by the minimum of one and the maximum of three. While the mixed/joint knowledge is a resources which is not supposed to achieve high synergies with a mean of 2.75. Also the maximum reflects this as firms saw very low potential for synergies and gave in consequence a five while the minimum is again one. The next resource is the *expertise of R&D personnel* which is not R&D specific. This resource is rated with less potential than the tangible resources, but nonetheless the mean of 2.33 is still a high potential for synergies. Again the extreme values reflect the mean with a minimum of one and a maximum of four. This is comparable to the *social/soft skills of R&D personnel* which are the next resource to be focused on. Here the minimum of one but especially the maximum of five reflects the low mean of 2.56 which is an average potential for synergies. The last four intangible resources can be subsumed under organisational resources. Focusing on the *operational structure* which seems to deliver high potential synergies with a mean of 2.00. The minimum is one more time one while the maximum value is three. So this resource is up to now the intangible resource with the highest potential for synergies. The complete opposite is the *organisational structure* of a firm which seems to be the resource with the least potentials for synergies occurring with a mean of 2.78 and a minimum of one and a maximum of five. The last but one intangible resource is *external perception*. The potential synergies for this resource are high with a mean of 1.89 it is the second highest valuation. A minimum of one and a maximum of three support this valuation. Finally the *internal perception* with a mean of 2.11 is also a resource with high potentials for synergies. The extreme values are similar to the resource before. A good overview on the results is given in table 7-3.

	Potential Synergies for R&D Resources	Observations	Mean	Standard Deviation	Min	Max
1	General infrastructure	10	2.00	0.82	1	3
2	R&D infrastructure	10	1.80	0.63	1	3
3	R&D personnel (headcount)	10	2.20	0.79	1	4
4	External R&D knowledge	9	2.56	1.24	1	4
5	Internal R&D knowledge	9	2.11	0.78	1	3
6	Mixed/Joint knowledge	8	2.75	1.28	1	5
7	Expertise of R&D personnel (not R&D specific)	9	2.33	1.00	1	4
8	Social/Soft skills of R&D personnel	9	2.55	1.13	1	5
9	Operational structure	9	2.00	0.87	1	3
10	Organisational structure	9	2.78	1.30	1	5
11	External perception	9	1.89	0.78	1	3
12	Internal perception	9	2.11	0.78	1	3

Table 7-3 Potential synergies for R&D resources
Source: own Survey

Summarising the results of the potential synergies evaluated for each resource by this question results on the one hand in four resources which are valued with high synergy potential (2.00) or better (1,2,9 and11). While there also four resources which are identified with lower potentials than 2.5 for synergies than the other resources. So these resources have an average potential to raise synergies (4, 6, 8 and 10). It has again to be noted that this result can only give a ranking and not the absolute potential synergies or the difference in potential synergies between different resources. Nonetheless these results offer some interesting possibilities for a multivariate analysis. Beforehand there is a final question which has to be dealt with.

This last question is concerned about the **importance of resources to the success of R&D.** Comparing the number of observations with the preceding questions this is the only question where every resource is completely answered by all responding firms. The first resource is one more time the tangible resource *general infrastructure* that is according to the answers only of average importance for the success of R&D as the mean value is 2.91 part. This is also supported by the fact that the minimum is only a high importance which is the only resource where the minimum is not a one. The maximum is a four. In opposition to the general infrastructure the *R&D infrastructure* is situated with a high importance for the success of R&D. Hence the mean is 2.09 with a minimum of one and a maximum of three. Even more important is the last tangible resource measured through *R&D personnel* which was valued with a mean of 1.91. The extreme values are similar to the resource before which appears to be logical as the results are close together. However, analysing the missing intangible resource is in the centre of the following section. First the *external R&D knowledge* with a mean of 2.64 and a maximum of four shows that the importance is more of average degree. Nonetheless external R&D knowledge is in the group of resources which is in the middle between the most important and the least important resources. According to this survey the most important resource to the success of R&D is an intangible resource. The results indicate *internal R&D knowledge* with a mean of 1.64 and a maximum of three as most relevant. Nonetheless there are some more resources to be discussed. There is also the mixed/joint knowledge with a mean of 2.36 with close extreme values of one and three. In opposition to this explicit and specific knowledge the tacit or more general knowledge of the R&D personnel is not as important to the success as the three resources described before. Hence the mean for *not R&D specific expertise of R&D personnel* is 2.91 which is also reflected by the maximum of five. The *social/soft skill of R&D personnel* with a mean of 2.82 is of a little more importance also reflected by the maximum of four but still at the end of the mid field of important resources to the success of R&D. Analysing the operational structure the results are similar to the soft skills discussed before in all details. The *organisational structure* is the resource with the least importance for success of R&D with a mean of 3.09. Important to note in this case is especially the maximum which is four so this result seems to reflect a very widespread opinion. Another resource, which is given an average degree of importance for the success of R&D, is the external perception with a mean of 3.00. The maximum for this resource is five. Finally there is the internal perception with a mean of 2.45 and a maximum of four which is a result for the upper mid field. An overview on the data discussed before can be found in table 7-4.

	Importance of Resources for Success of R&D	Observations	Mean	Standard Deviation	Min	Max
1	General infrastructure	11	2.91	0.83	2	4
2	R&D infrastructure	11	2.09	0.54	1	3
3	R&D personnel (headcount)	11	1.91	0.70	1	3
4	External R&D knowledge	11	2.64	0.92	1	4
5	Internal R&D knowledge	11	1.64	0.67	1	3
6	Mixed/Joint knowledge	11	2.36	0.67	1	3
7	Expertise of R&D personnel (not R&D specific)	11	2.91	1.04	1	5
8	Social/Soft skills of R&D personnel	11	2.82	0.98	1	4
9	Operational structure	11	2.82	0.75	1	4
10	Organisational structure	11	3.09	0.94	1	4
11	External perception	11	3.00	1.26	1	5
12	Internal perception	11	2.45	0.82	1	4

Table 7-4 Importance of resources for success of R&D
Source: own Survey

Summarising the results of this questions leads to one central difference to the other questions. In this case the results have a wider spread from 1.64 to 3.09 which did not occur in the questions discussed before so there seems to be a different importance between resources which seems to be more easily to identify. Or another reason might be that the sources for success are more general and in consequence are less dependent on the underlying firm and its specific characteristics. Nonetheless the results of this question give again on the one hand a group of three recourses (2, 3 and 5) that are more important than others. On the other hand there are four resources which are suggested to be of less importance than the other resources (1, 7, 10 and 11). Some further analyses are necessary for a more detailed view on the picture developing. This will be part of the multivariate analysis performed in the following chapter to point out at some relationships.

7.2.2 MULTIVARIATE DATA ANALYSIS

Subsequently to the prior conducted univariate data analysis, this book compiles also multivariate analysis to address and to investigate more complex relations between different dimensions and resources. This procedure will offer a plain view on the resource base of R&D units. The primary target of this section will be the assessment of the developed hypothesises. The presented analysis has been based on the results of the univariate data analysis. Hence, the attributes of single resources will be used from this prior section.

This book will use regression methods to highlight the relations between the different resources described above. In addition to this statistical scheme the single resources will be clustered in order to classify similar resources. This approach will help to gain a detailed view on the nature of the relevant resources for R&D.

This book compiles a regression analysis based on the Ordinary Least Squares method. This approach is going to address the dependence of one variable from another one. The regression model builds on linear relationships between the different variables.[563] The quality of this regression can be judged through the analysis of the appearance of significance levels. These levels have to be addressed especially during this evaluation as the underlying sample is very small.

A second method used by this book has been the hierarchical cluster analysis. This approach seems to be necessary to extract relevant classes of resources, based on statistical models.[564] This will provide profound information about arising classes of resources.[565] Interpreting the results of the conducted survey will therefore rely on robust mathematical models. Hence, the quality of the discussion

---

[563] See Stier (1999), p. 241.
[564] See Aldenderfer/Blashfield (1984), p. 19.
[565] See Brosius (2002), p. 627.

of results will be improved significantly. According to this approach, the Ward Method has been applied. The Ward Method can be structured as an agglomerative cluster approach. The key objective is to minimise the loss of homogeneity during the clustering of single variables. Although this method is only applicable for metric scales, the use of mean values offers the possibility to apply this cluster analysis on the available variables and results.[566] In the light of the wide range of cluster methods, the results of the Ward Method have been crosschecked with the average linkage method. The use of different methods will support the quality of the results of this evaluation.

The following sub-chapters will outline the results of the multivariate analysis according to the prior discussed hypothesises (cf. chapter 6.2.4). In consequence the relation between relatedness and synergies will be discussed first.

7.2.2.1 RELATEDNESS AND POTENTIAL SYNERGIES

The basic consideration of the RBV, stressing the relationship between resources relatedness and synergies, has been tested with this hypothesis. The impact of relatedness on the potential synergies will be assessed. Relatedness will be classified as the independent variable in this model. The potential synergies arising from this relatedness will be classified as the dependent variable. For both variables, means have been calculated during the univariate analysis. Combining these two dimensions through a linear regression model, relying on fitted values, will offer the following view on the impact of relatedness on the appearance of potential synergies as shown with figure 7-6.

---

[566] See Stier (1999), p. 336.

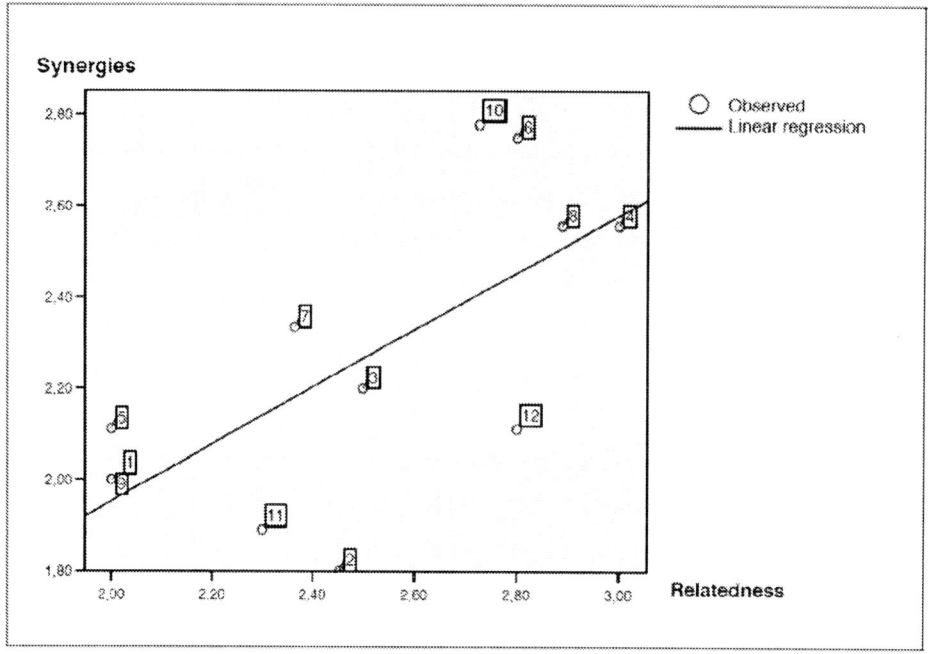

Figure 7-6 Linear regression between relatedness and potential synergies
Source: own survey

The linear regression builds on a constant factor of 0.701 and a slope of 0.626. This model shows a significant relationship between relatedness and synergies. Supported and illustrated by the p-level of 0.015. Thus the relationship can be interpreted as statistically significant, based on the underlying sample.

In order to classify the resources in terms of their relatedness and potential synergies, a cluster analysis has been performed. The Ward Method provided a first cluster containing the resources 1, 5 and 9. The second cluster compiles of the resources 2, 3, 7, 11 and 12. The third cluster represents the resources 4, 6, 8 and 10. Using average linkage for clustering will provide quite similar results. The clustering can be visualised according to the following figure:

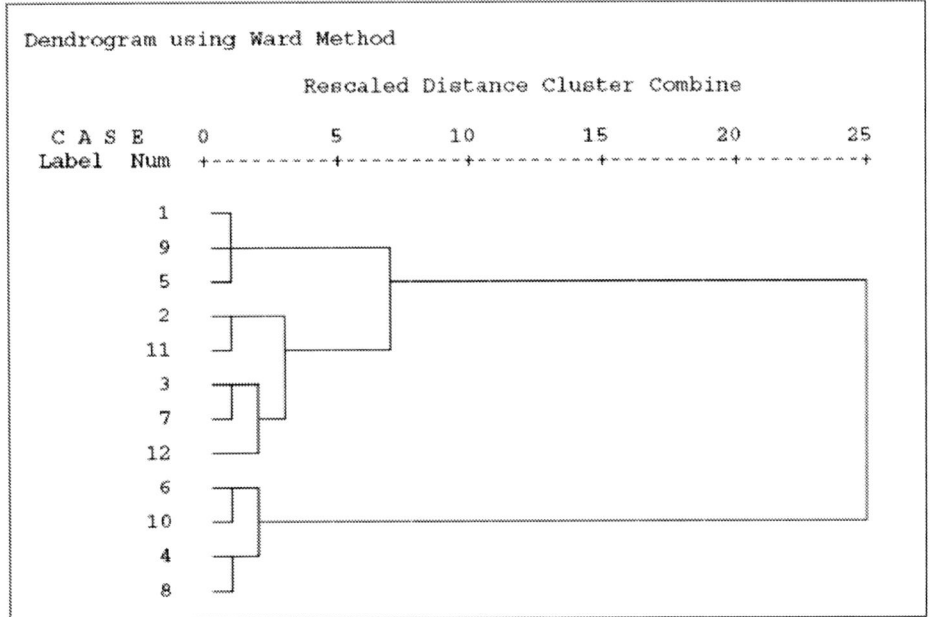

Figure 7-7 Dendrogram – relatedness and potential synergies

Source: own survey

Analysing the relationship between relatedness and potential synergies, the investigated sample provided proof for the basic assumption of the RBV. Relatedness can be described as a major source for the existence of synergies. However, the sample provided an insight into the resource base of R&D units. These resources can be structured with different degrees of relatedness and therefore different synergy potentials. Based on the answers of the conducted questionnaire, three resources seem to offer superior relatedness and therefore superior potential synergies. These resources are: general infrastructure (1), internal R&D knowledge (5) and operational structure (9). Resources offering only low relatedness are, based on this sample, external R&D knowledge (4), mixed/joint R&D knowledge (6), social/soft skills of R&D personnel (8) and organisational structure (10). Resources with medium relatedness consequently offer only average potential synergies. These resources are R&D infrastructure (2), expenditures for human resources in R&D (3), expertise of R&D personnel (unspecific) (7), external perception of the company (image, brands) (11) and culture of the firm (12).

Interpretation

The high relatedness of general infrastructure is following the general interpretation of these assets. General infrastructure is highly unspecific from an R&D specific point of view. Unspecific resources can easily be used across different BUs or even different functional areas. In addition, these kinds of resources also increase the potential synergies through low potential dissynergies.[567] Different R&D units can access these resources independently of their scope of research. Hence it seems quite obvious that general infrastructure offers a high grade of relatedness and consequently high potential synergies.

The high relatedness of internal R&D knowledge offers not a similar plain interpretation. Especially, in combination of the results for external and joint knowledge, the results of this sample might offer a wide area of arguments. Although the used sample seems to be too narrow to give general explanations, this result might explain the strategic approach for the assessment of key technologies. Firms concentrate on a few strategic technologies and capabilities. They build their business lines and BUs along these key resources.[568] Hence, the BUs all access a similar technological knowledge base. This knowledge will be provided through internal R&D efforts. In consequence, internal R&D knowledge will be related across different BUs and consequently offers high potential synergies. Following these arguments, external and joint knowledge will only be applied in minor areas or as additional resources in specific R&D units. Hence, the rating of these resources as relatively unrelated and low potential synergies will be the logical consequence from this point of view. These arguments have not only been formulated in the relevant literature[569], but have also been confirmed during discussions with various R&D managers from the interviewed firms.

A similar ambivalent result can be found with structural resources. On the one hand, operational structures have been rated as related and offering high potential synergies. On the other hand, organisational structures have been rated as relatively unrelated and low potential synergies. This seems surprising because of the numerous papers pronouncing the relevance of organisational structure of

---

[567] See Szeless (2001), p. 36.
[568] See Taylor (1990), p. 102.
[569] See e.g. Lynseky (1999), Quelling (2000) or Taylor (1990).

R&D within a firm.[570] The result of this survey however, focuses more on the relevance of operational structures. This might be comprehensive as operational aspects affect R&D processes directly on unit level. Hence, the different attitude about structural resources seems to be understandable.

Quite straightforward information about potential synergies can be taken from the kind of resources offering the highest relatedness. On the one hand, resources offer a high relatedness if they are most unspecific like general resources, but also R&D infrastructure in general or the expenditures for human resources in R&D. On the other hand, resources offer high potential synergies, if they are connected with the internal R&D process itself. This can be found with the resources internal R&D knowledge and operational structure and as well as with the expertise of R&D personnel (not R&D specific).

Although the results of every single resource offer different interpretations, it has to be acknowledged, that relatedness can be classified as a major source for the generation of synergies. Three specific resources offer a higher relatedness and therefore might be able to generate more synergies. These results support the basic approach of this book, as a detailed resource analysis might be necessary to judge the interactions and correlations between different R&D units correctly. However, apart from the correlation of relatedness and synergies, the actual relevance of resources for the R&D process has to be acknowledged separately. Resources might offer high potential synergies but might not be relevant for the success of R&D efforts. In order to value resources in R&D properly, a second dimension has to be applied on the resource base of R&D. Hence, this book conducts this analysis in the following chapter to complete the view on resources in R&D.

7.2.2.2 SYNERGIES AND RELEVANCE OF RESOURCES IN R&D

The second dimension within this resource analysis is going to address the relevance of single resources for the R&D process itself. However, as this book addresses the analysis of relatedness within R&D, this dimension merely acts as a

---

[570] See Argyres/Silverman (2004), p. 929, Kuemmerle (1998), p. 111.

control account for the valuation of the prior conducted results. Hence, the major information based on this result will be if resources with high potential synergies will be rated with special relevance for the success of R&D. The underlying assumption is that the realisation of synergies should be the major objective for diversified firms.[571] Hence, in diversified companies, resource relatedness should be accountable for the overall success of R&D across businesses. The results from the underlying sample however, give a quite differentiated view of the relationship between potential synergies and relevance for the R&D success.

This dimension has been modelled with potential synergies as the independent variable and the relevance for the success of R&D as the dependent variable. The sample has been analysed with a similar regression model as applied above. Again, this statistical model relies on the mean results of the univariate analysis. The results of this analysis are outlined in the following figure:

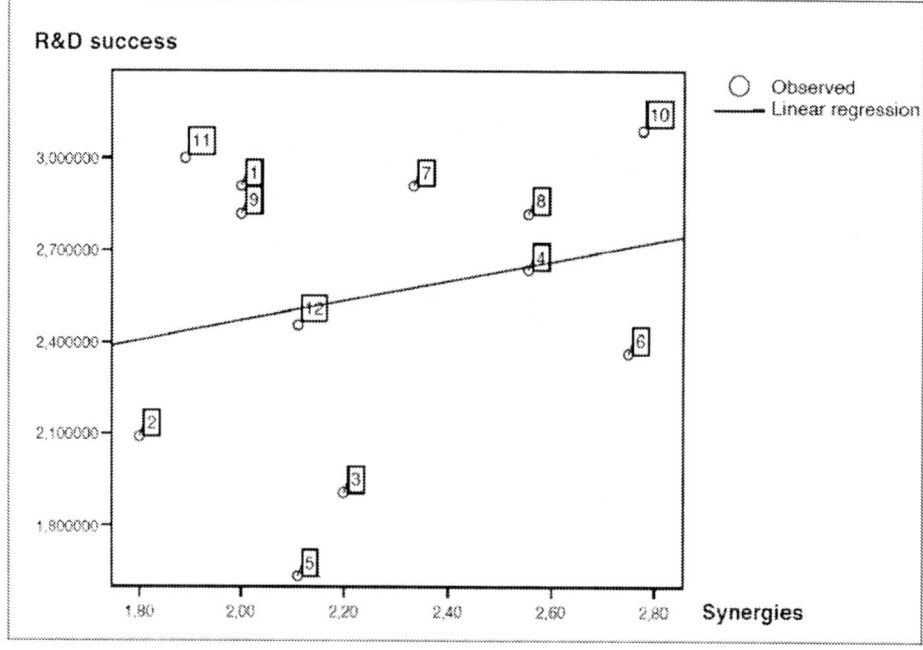

Figure 7-8 Linear regression between potential synergies and R&D success

Source: own survey

---

[571] See e.g. Del Canto/Gonzalez (1999), p. 891.

The regression analysis conducted a linear function with a constant factor of 1.832 and a slope of 0.985. Although the regression method conducted a linear relation between potential synergies and success of R&D, this relationship has to be questioned. Based on the given sample, the statistical model has not been able to give significant results. The p-level only accounts for 0.477 and therefore, the results of this study cannot be rated as statistically significant. However, this significance does not enunciate a missing relationship between potential synergies and relevance for the R&D process, but merely pronounce a too narrow sample to conduct such results with sufficient reliability.[572]

Structuring the resources according to the prior used cluster methods will give a detailed view about different classes of resources. The following figure outlines the results of a cluster analysis using the Ward Method. Again, other methods produced similar results.

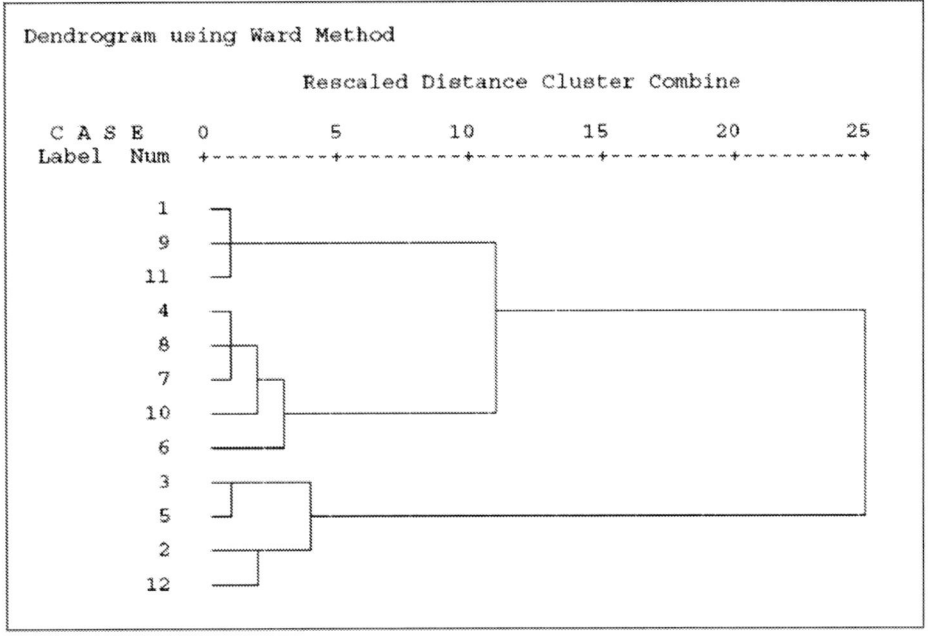

Figure 7-9 Dendrogram – potential synergies and R&D success
Source: own survey

---

[572] See Stier (1999), p. 156.

The structure from this cluster analysis revealed an interesting view on the relationship between potential synergies of resources and their relevance for the R&D process. The investigated assumption of a relationship between potential synergies and the relevance of single resources might not be answered through this sample. However, a number of resources offer relative high potential synergies and as well as a high relevance for R&D. These resources are: R&D infrastructure (2), Expenditures for human resources in R&D (3), Internal R&D knowledge (5) and culture of the firm (12). Internal R&D knowledge has already been rated high in relatedness and consequently high for potential synergies. Although the resources have not achieved the highest rating in relatedness, they contribute meaningfully to the R&D process. Support for the relation between synergies and relevance can be found with the results for the resources offering only low potential synergies as well as low relevance for R&D. These resources are: external R&D knowledge (4), mixed/joint knowledge (6), expertise of R&D personnel (7) and organisational structure (10). However, three resources offer high potential synergies but do not contribute to the success of R&D processes. These resources are: general infrastructure (1), operational structure (9) and external image of the firm (11). These results indicate a more complex relationship between this two analysed dimensions and support the conducted approach of a detailed resource-by-resource analysis.

Interpretation

Interpreting the results presented during this analysis has to acknowledge the weaknesses of the underlying sample. The low number of answering firms has not led to statistically significant results for this dimension and hypothesis. However, following a straight descriptive data approach, the results might offer an additional view on the resource base of R&D units and the interactions and interdependencies between single resources.

The first cluster of resources (1, 9 and 11) outlines a basic problem of the underlying research assumption. The coherence between relatedness, synergies and success cannot be found with these resources. All three resources offer high potential synergies but do not contribute to the success of R&D. This might be interpreted in the sense of resource attributes. These resources do not affect the

R&D process directly and therefore they might offer potential synergies and hence cost advantages through the realisation of different economics. However, they are not crucial for R&D projects but merely affect the environment of corporate R&D. Similar to these resources, the second cluster consists of resources offering neither potential synergies nor relevance for the R&D process. These resources already have been described above during the analysis of relatedness and synergies. These resources are not relevant for the R&D process and offer only low potential synergies. As argued above, these resources, especially external and joint knowledge resources, might be rated accordingly as they are usually not at central processes during R&D projects but are used occasionally whenever R&D units demand additional external resources.[573]

The third cluster offers another interesting view on the relevance of different resources. These resources offer high potential synergies and are also of utter importance for the success of R&D. All of these three resources are strongly related to core R&D aspects. They conclude three different dimensions including the material infrastructure, the R&D personnel and also the relevant internal knowledge. They represent the core elements of the R&D process. Therefore the basic assumption of the RBV and the relationship relatedness – synergies – success cannot be assumed undifferentiated for R&D units. To address the success dimensions within R&D resources properly, the nature of the analysed resources has to be acknowledged. Hence, the analysis of the resource relatedness, as conducted during the above-described dimensions, has to bear in mind the classification of the resources in question within the R&D environment.

The conducted multivariate analysis provided useful insights into the nature of the resource base of R&D units. In addition to the univariate analysis the multivariate part has been able to connect different dimensions in the view on single resources and offers a more detailed valuation of the relatedness concept of the RBV. This book was able to prove the significant relationship between relatedness and potential synergies based on the underlying sample. In addition the connection to a success dimension offered supplementary information which is useful to class the results of the prior conducted analysis. Hence, the major objectives of this

---

[573] See the arguments in Fritsch/Lukas (2001), p. 297.

book have been achieved and an applicable cross-check has been provided. The analysis outlined the most relevant resources in terms of relatedness and potential synergies. This book will use the gained knowledge about related resources to construct a measure of relatedness in the following chapter.

8 MODELLING RELATEDNESS OF R&D

Based on the results of the prior performed analysis of relatedness in R&D, this book is going to develop a measurement concept in order to give a framework for the assessment of relatedness of R&D units. In this chapter the concept will be outlined. The first part of this chapter will give an introduction into the basic principles, the reasons and the main objectives of this approach. In a second step, the analytical part of this approach will be described. In this part, the most relevant resources for R&D relatedness will be analysed in more detail. Afterwards, the results of this analysis will be used to construct a wholesale measurement concept in order to determine one final relatedness value. This ratio will aggregate the information about single resources and offers the possibility to find a clear proposition about the relatedness of the analysed R&D units of different firms or BUs.

8.1 BASIC CONSIDERATIONS

The main objective of this book has been the assessment of the relatedness of R&D. The arguments of the RBV led to an analysis of single resource relatedness. This view offered detailed insights into the nature of resources but is not able to reveal information about the overall relatedness. However, the analysis of R&D units will have to rely on the possibility to offer a clear statement about the final interpretation of resource relatedness. This additional perspective will be the focus of the presented framework. Based on the prior conducted research, the three most relevant resources will be analysed on a more detailed sub-level. Hence, the resources will be structured further. The main objective of this approach is the development of a concept which is able to combine the results of resource relatedness with each other and to give a weighted general result. Therefore, the results of this model will be explicit and will classify the analysed R&D units as related or unrelated. This method will be structured as an individual measurement concept for firms to analyse their existing cross-functional R&D relatedness or to assess potential future R&D partners. Hence, it will be applicable for the analysis of firms, regardless of size, industry focus and organisation. The concept is trying to be facile to understand, easy to apply and finally to offer reliable results for the users. To achieve these objectives, the concept has to build on more specified information about the three most relevant resources for relatedness. For this reason, the resources in question will be analysed in more detail throughout the next chapter.

8.2 IDENTIFICATION OF THE RELEVANT RESOURCES

As already introduced before, the three resource blocks with a high relatedness are in the centre of the following analysis. For this reason each of the resources is opened up on a more detailed sub-level for direct measurement of relatedness. In consequence a couple of resources are going to be identified on this more detailed level. The resource categories in the following chapters are basically trying to give a complete picture of the most important resources that can be subsumed under each of the three resources identified before. First the general infrastructure is in the centre of discussion, the second resource is the R&D specific internal knowledge and finally the operational structure is defined.

8.2.1 ANALYSING GENERAL INFRASTRUCTURE

As already mentioned in chapter 4.1.1.1 the general infrastructure or tangible assets appear to be a very large block where it seems to be very difficult to point out some resources at first sight. The fragmentation used in the introduction into mobile and immobile general infrastructure is for this measurement concept too rough especially as not all resources can be classified clearly in one of these groups. Hence there is a strong need for a more detailed fragmentation of the general infrastructure. The following analysis is based on the German commercial codes (HGB) which offer a relatively detailed classification of the tangible assets of a firm.[574] The first resource of which the general resources consist can be described as **real estate and building**. These immovable resources are torn together because of the legal status which is based on the HGB that advices to show these resources in one position.[575] Secondly the **technical equipment and machinery** can be identified as a part of the general infrastructure. These resources might be movable or immovable so that there is no clear classification in

---

[574] See HGB (2006), §§266II and 240 III.
[575] See Peemöller (2003), p.89.

this context.[576] Nonetheless this classification makes sense as it reflects a second large part of the general resources. In this context it seems important to note that the technical equipment and machinery discussed is explicitly **not** directly connected with R&D. Finally the last resource completing the general resources are **other assets, furniture and office equipment**. This resource contains all the necessary fundamentals which are important to run a business. Figure 8-1 gives a visual overview on the three characteristic specifications of the general resources.

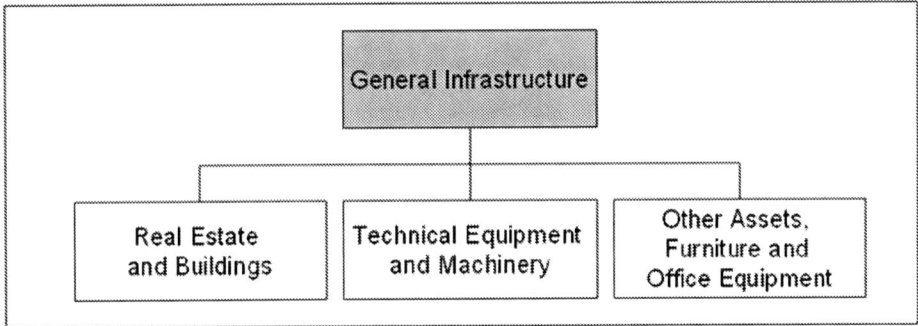

Figure 8-1 Detailed Categorisation of general Resources
Source: Following HGB (2006) §§266 II and 240 III.

After analysing and defining the general infrastructure the next paragraph will focus on R&D specific internal knowledge and a detailed analysis.

8.2.2 ANALYSIS OF INTERNAL R&D KNOWLEDGE

The research conducted knowledge found internal R&D knowledge as one of the most relevant resources for the determination of relatedness of R&D units. To further structure this key resource, this book will rely on the most basic views on internal available knowledge in corporations. As described in chapter 4.1 (A), R&D knowledge can be distinguished according to its occurrence i.e. knowledge can be distinguished into explicit and tacit knowledge.

---

[576] See Peemöller (2003), p.90.

On the one hand, knowledge is available as securitised assets through patents and copyrights[577] or through unprotected but nevertheless openly available through internal date like white papers, handbooks, data stocks and other.[578] This kind of knowledge can be described as explicit and can be assessed easily through the available data of different R&D sites. Also, the available knowledge in one R&D site can be easily transferred to another one, as the company holds the full rights on this intellectual property. Additionally, intellectual property rights can be valuated through different approaches, known e.g. from the financial accounting perspective.[579] For the sake of this book and the analysis on this detailed sub-level, a distinction between legally protected knowledge and unprotected knowledge seems applicable. Hence the measurement concept will rely on two further classes of explicit knowledge. However, these rights have to be assessed in detail to reveal their possible contribution to relatedness. The same approach has to be followed with other internal knowledge available. The internal knowledge stock has to be relevant for different R&D units in order to generate possible relatedness and synergies. Hence, a detailed analysis of the relevant property rights and knowledge seems to be necessary. Although this information might offer easy access, the relatedness valuation has to be assessed by adequate experts and has to be conducted on the basis of case studies to acknowledge individual circumstances.

On the other hand, internal R&D knowledge is available from R&D personnel. Scientists, engineers and other researchers contribute their individual knowledge to the research activities of their R&D unit. This knowledge, however, is tacit and therefore not available for an easy access valuation. The firm cannot easy access this knowledge as it is bounded to individuals. In consequence, a transfer of this knowledge might be difficult or even impossible.[580] Nevertheless, these resources are often the most relevant for the performance of R&D.[581] Hence; these important resources have to be acknowledged and have to be accessed with special attention. This kind of knowledge has to be relevant for more than one R&D site to be able to be valued as related. That means that different R&D units have to rely

---

[577] See Pike et al. (2005), p. 113.
[578] See Tolbert et al. (2002), p. 467.
[579] See Peemöller (2003), p.89.
[580] See Del Canto and Gonzalez (1999), p. 897.
[581] See Teece (1980), p. 223.

e.g. on the same kind of engineers working in related scientific areas. Therefore, different R&D sites have to be analysed according to their personnel and underlying scientific discipline. Again, a possible approach might be the valuation through adequate experts within the structure of individual case studies. The structure of internal R&D knowledge has been outlined in the following figure:

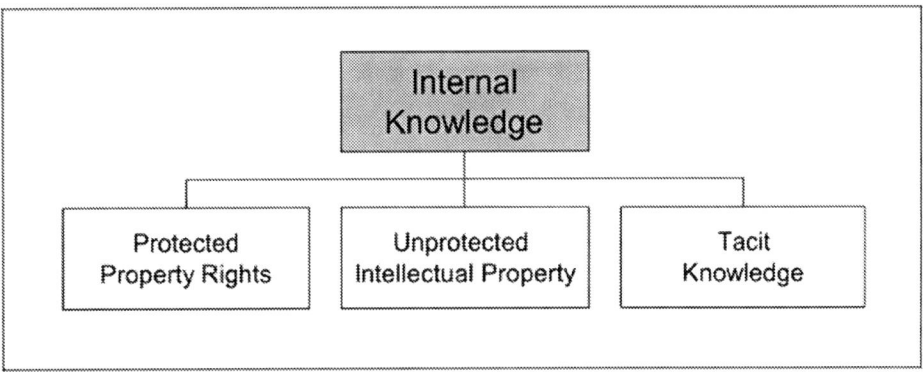

Figure 8-2 Detailed categorisation of internal knowledge
Source: based on Del Canto and Gonzalez (1999), p. 897.

8.2.3 ANALYSING THE OPERATIONAL STRUCTURE

In the beginning it is necessary to recapitulate the position of the operational structure within the resource base developed in chapter 4.1.2.2. Hence the operational structure can be classified as intangible resource. Further it belongs to the group of organisational resources and within these to the structure based resources. This resource is as almost all the intangible resources difficult to describe or measure precisely as there are several different characteristics which might be used. The literature offers a few concepts to characterise processes.[582] Hence this book chose a general categorisation for obvious complexity reasons. The following analysis is therefore based on a structure developed by FORTE. This categorisation identifies three different types of processes. First there are the so called **primary processes** which are basically concerned with goods and services on the one hand and with order processing on the other hand. Some examples with no claim for completeness are production and customer service

---

[582] See Heilmann (1996), pp.92.

processes on the side of goods and services or sales, distribution and market communication processes on the side of order processing.[583] These primary processes are often described as the core processes of a company which is basically resulting from the contact to external customers that is characteristic to a large extent. In general these processes are of operative nature.[584] The second types of processes which are identified are **secondary processes**. In this case the theory draws a distinction between operational processes and management processes.[585] The occurring problems, derived by this separation, are not discussed in more detail. This book suggests according to the literature that operational processes are widely standardised so that in consequence management processes are not so relevant. Otherwise this separation would be problematic. A few examples for management processes are strategic planning and human resource management while examples for operational processes are financial accounting and information supply.[586] At this point it is important to note that management processes are not connected or related to management capabilities, referring to chapter 4.1.1. Finally there are **innovation processes** which are again described by operational processes and management processes. An example for management processes is the so called management of innovation while two examples for operational resources are the product development and the process optimisation.[587] These categories are visualised in Figure 8-3.

---

[583] See Forte (2002), p.27.
[584] See Forte (2002), pp.25-26.
[585] See Forte (2002), p.27.
[586] See Forte (2002), pp.25-27.
[587] See Forte (2002), p.27.

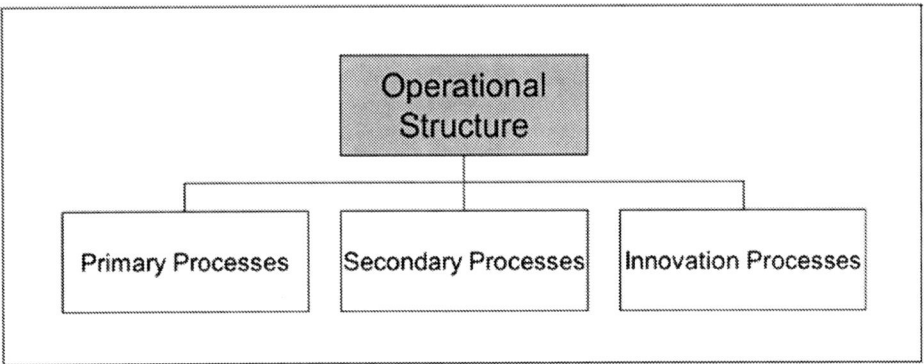

Figure 8-3 Detailed categorisation of operational structure
Source: based on Forte (2002), p. 27.

8.3 MEASUREMENT CONCEPT

Based on the analysis of the three relevant resources, this book operationalises a measurement concept in order to structure the assessment of relatedness in R&D. This concept will aggregate information about the relatedness of single resource aspects to a top-level measure and is therefore able to give a clear answer on the resource analysis of R&D units. It is structured as a two-level concept. Level one will include the three most relevant resources as well as the summary position of other resources. These other resources have been rated as not relevant through the analysis conducted above. This book, however, will include these dimensions to build a complete picture on the resource base of R&D, but as a consequence of the prior results, will not force a detailed analysis of the whole range of resources. Level two will offer a more detailed view on the three resources discussed. This will provide additional insights into these crucial resources and will offer superior results of the investigation of relatedness. Together, this two level information can be summarised into an overall relatedness value of the analysed R&D units. Hence, the concept can be used to generate a profound statement about the relatedness of two or more R&D units. Before applying this concept Figure 8-4 gives a first overview on the two level concept. The application of this measurement concept is discussed in the following paragraph.

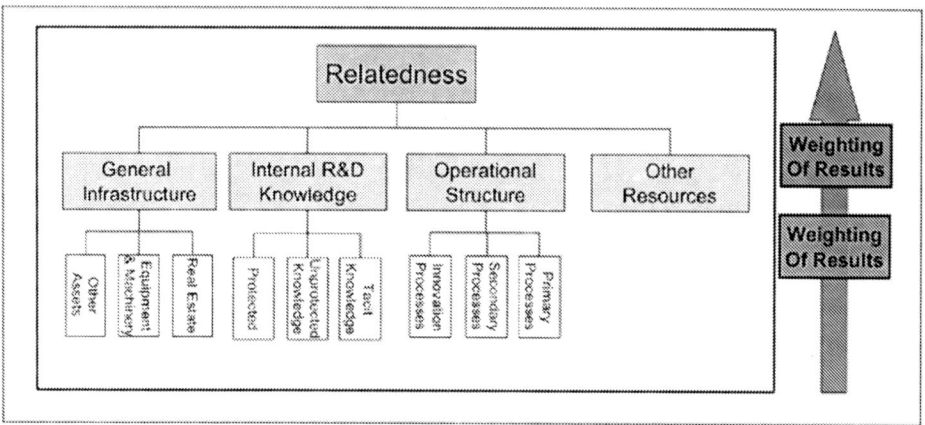

Figure 8-4 Overview measurement concept

Source: own development

In a first step, the analysts performing this analysis are asked to rate the relative importance of the single resource of a sub-level e.g. technical equipment and machinery or tacit knowledge in relation to the resource in question e.g. general infrastructure or internal R&D knowledge. The value of the individual sub-levels will account for 100% within every resource. This structure will represent the individual situation and environment of the analysed corporations and R&D units. Hence, the analysis has to be performed by a qualified expert, who is able to apply this concept to the analysed firms. Afterwards, the relatedness of each sub-category will have to be rated on a range between total unrelatedness (0), very low relatedness (1), low relatedness (2), common relatedness (3), high relatedness (4) and very high relatedness (5). This scale opens a wide range of possible interpretation. Hence a more detailed description seems to be necessary. This book proposes the following narrow definition: (0) all or the overwhelming part of resources offer no similarity and no traceable relatedness, (1) only very few aspects of the analysed resource can be interpreted as related, (2) some but still the minority of resources offer joint usage, (3) average relatedness based on similarities between R&D units based on the general similarity of R&D units, (4) substantially more resources offer the possibility of joint use, the R&D units complement each other within this special resource and (5) the overwhelming majority of resources can be described as related and the R&D units might act as a symbioses within this resource.

Together with the prior created weighting the relatedness value of this resource can be produced. Applying this procedure on the other resources will lead to a relatedness result for every resource. These findings can be interpreted individually to give answers for the sources of relatedness between the analysed R&D units. However, to be able to give answers about the overall relatedness, a further aggregation is necessary and can be interpreted as the summary of level one results. Figure 8-5 visualises the first described measurement step of the process.

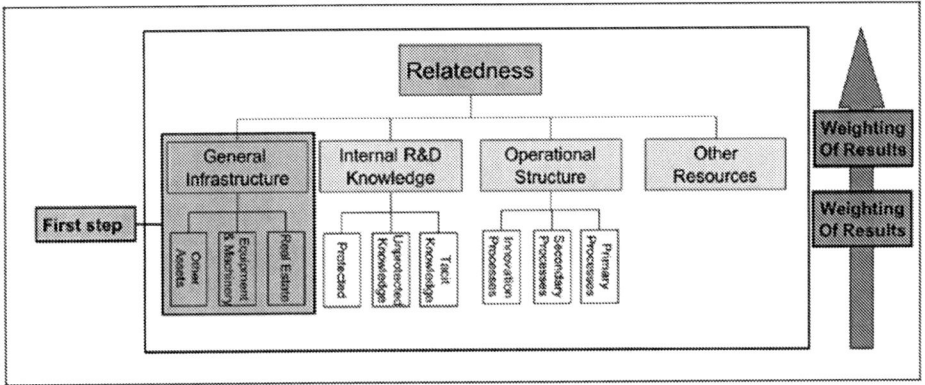

Figure 8-5 First step within the measurement concept

Source: own development

In a second step, the analysts will be asked to develop an additional weighting system for the four resource categories (general resources, operational structure, internal R&D knowledge and other resources). The value of these weightings will also sum up to 100%. The prior developed relatedness results of the sub-level will be weighted with these factors to produce a final overall relatedness value. For the summary position 'other resources' the relatedness score has to be developed similar to the above described first step, but without the otherwise used sub-categories. However, if the analysis of the underlying R&D units will lead to other estimations about the relevance of this other resources, as has been presumed with this concept, a more detailed investigation into these other resources will be necessary.[588] The second step is visualised in Figure 8-6.

---

[588] Based on the previously discussed analysis of the resource base of R&D units, this situation seems to be not a likely estimation. However, as this concept should be open for unknown

Finally, the four relative scores will be summed up for a final value of relatedness of the analysed R&D units. This final score visualises the relatedness based on the analysed resources and can be interpreted as a measure of the resource fit of R&D units. The structure of this concept is outlined in the following figure:

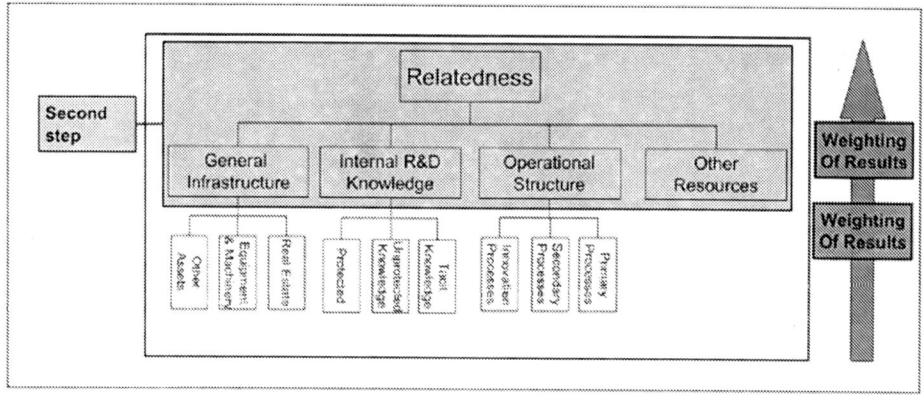

Figure 8-6 Second step within the measurement concept

Source: own development

To support a plain view on the potential success of R&D cooperation, the results of this measurement concept can and should be clustered. This book proposes the following clusters:[589]

Values between 0 and 2.5 should be interpreted as unrelated R&D units. The cooperation between R&D units will not lead to a rising overall success and even might lead to negative effects.[590]

Values between 2.5 and 3.5 should be interpreted as neither related nor unrelated R&D units. A clear statement about success contributions from cooperation will not be possible. However, the potential of positive effects will be very low from a resource-based point of view.

Values above 3.5 should be interpreted as related R&D units. The resources of different sites will complement each other and cooperation offers high potential

---

resource constellations, this scenario should be part of the possible considerations during the analysis of R&D units.

[589] These clusters are based on the empirical analysis of the results of the survey as described above. Although this measurement concept uses a different scale, the results should be clustered accordingly to these results as they have been found as statistically significant. See chapter 7.3.

[590] Negative effects might arise from the occurrence of dissynergies. See chapter 4.4.

synergies. The risk of negative success contributions can be assumed as being low.

Analysis following this structure and this concept will not be able to replace a detailed investigation about the relation between R&D units which might include e.g. strategic consideration. However, this approach will be able to give clear results for the valuation of resource relatedness and therefore should be a central part of relation contemplations about R&D units. Results from this approach will give clear answers according to the three classes outlined above. The analyst will be able to build a clear statement about the resource relatedness of R&D units.

For a better understanding and in order to offer a possibility how this measurement could be performed in practice, the concept is modelled as a compact one page comprising hand leaflet. Assessing the relatedness of R&D within a firm by using this form would probably help to identify relevant and irrelevant resources. The hand leaflet has to be worked through from the left to the right hand side and comprises the whole steps described before, which finally lead to an overall relatedness value of the analysed R&D department.

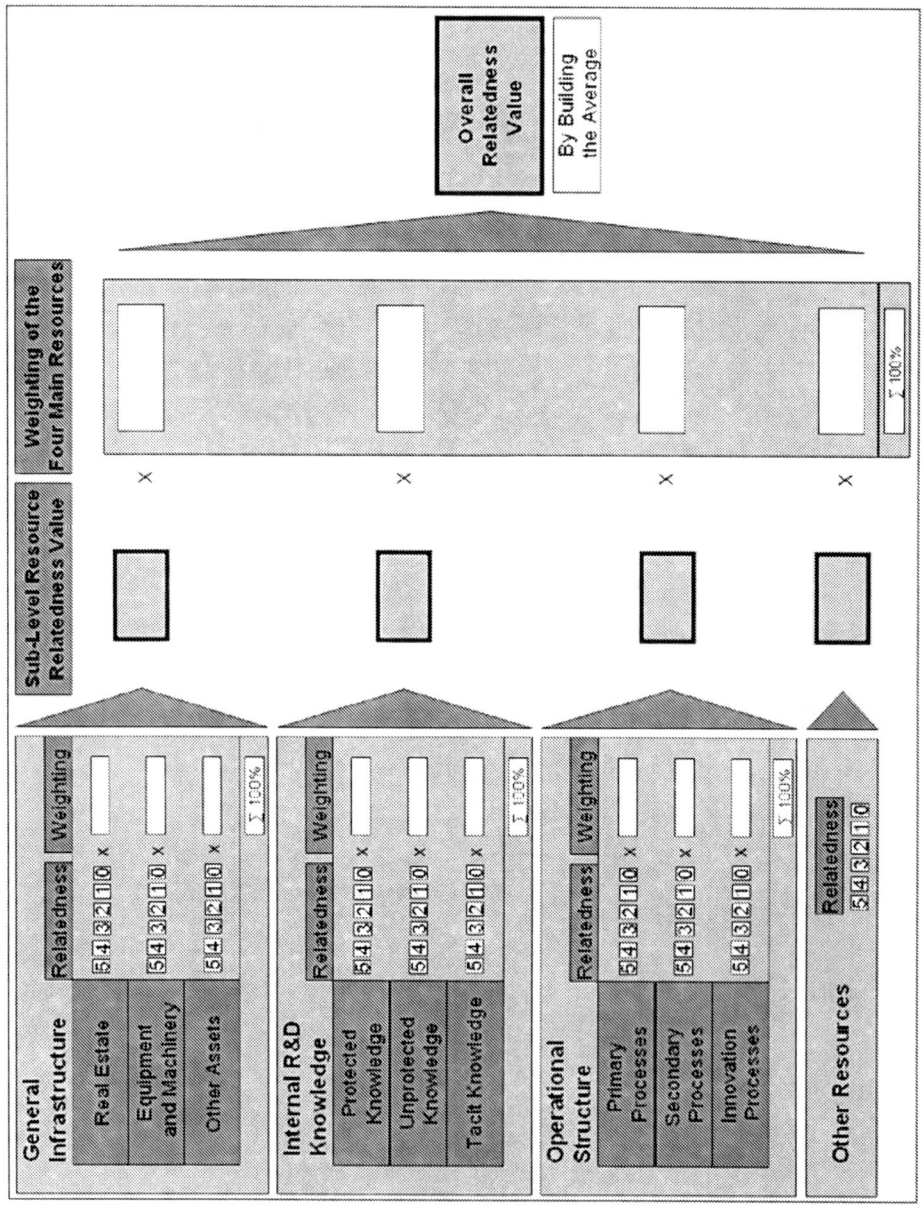

Figure 8-7 Hand leaflet for measuring relatedness in R&D

Source: own development

9 CONCLUSION

Whether and how diversified firms benefit from their different BUs is one of the most enduring questions discussed in strategic management research. Today, nearly all published papers acknowledge the relevance of the RBV for a correct assessment of this strategic question. Hence the arguments for diversification and MBFs have to build on resource relatedness in order to gain super benefits compared to single business solutions. These additional payoffs might be realised through the achievement of economics of scope and scale. This ongoing discussion structures the motives for diversification as well as for analysis of MBFs.

Analysing diversification mainly follows a single resource perspective. TANRIVERDI might be used as an example of state-of-the-art authors addressing this kind of research.[591] This book sought to follow a different approach. The main objective had been the analysis of a single functional unit and its underlying resource base. This single functional entity had been R&D as this can be interpreted as one of the core functions within the firm. The future success relies on the capability of R&D units to generate future business opportunities. Hence, diversified firm have to generate at least equal future potentials as comparable single units. Based on the importance of R&D, the analysis of resource relatedness within R&D seems quite logical. In addition, during the assessment of R&D relatedness, the concentration on single resources does not seem to reflect the complex resource structure of R&D units. Therefore, the analysis has to include the whole resource base at least during the first steps of the examination. For a successful attempt of analysing R&D a profound understanding of the research object has to be developed. This necessary information environment has been build during chapter 3. This had been the basis for the development of the resource base of R&D units which had been central for most parts of this book. The resource base is constraint on R&D specific resources and in consequence excludes financial resources. As a consequence, this structure of resources had been constructed on a more detailed level as usually can be found in published

---

[591] Tanriverdi and others is publishing on a wide area of resources. However, their methodological approach focuses on single resources. See chapter 5.1.

research papers. Hence, the structure is one of the key contributions of this book to research and also a methodological example used by a number of other diploma theses written in a similar context.

The prior developed resource base of R&D has been the basis for the conception of the synergy model also performed during chapter 4. R&D units are able to benefit from resource relatedness and therefore are able to generate higher outputs from their research or are able to reduce research costs. The realisation of synergies depends on the joint use of resources in the case of tangible resources or on the transfer of resources in the case of intangible resources. However, the positive effects of resource relatedness have to exceed the negative effects of diversification, which have been described as dissynergies. These negative aspects are based on knowledge-related, cognitive-related or cultural-related problems. Hence, firms have to bear in mind to assess negative aspects as well. However, the analysis of overall corporate success due to relatedness has not been the scope of this study. Moreover, this book focuses on the evaluation of relatedness between R&D units based on resources as this approach might build a first and important step during the analysis of diversified firms.

To structure and to evaluate the developed resource base, an empirical survey has been conducted. The results of the questionnaire have also been used as a crosscheck for the theoretical framework of this book and the assumptions of the resource based view. This part of the book builds on the results of already performed studies. Hence, the empirical approaches published in the past have been analysed. In this context, the usefulness of these concepts has been evaluated. The main results of this literature review has been the information that most of the used empirical approaches are build on a weak conceptual grounding and therefore are unable to investigate resource relatedness between different R&D units. Hence, this book sought to give an alternative approach for the measurement of relatedness and performed a statistical survey. The interviewed firms have all been large companies from German speaking countries and all of them are listed within DAX 30, MDAX, SDAX (DAX 120), TECDAX, ATX Prime and SMI. Most of the listed firms have reached a corporate size which indicates multiple BUs. Therefore, most of these corporations have been relevant for this survey, excluding non-R&D performing corporations. Although the response rate of relevant corporations has been very low, the results of this questionnaire have been able to give additional information based on the outcomes of a descriptive analysis. This book therefore has been able to confirm the basic assumptions of the RBV. One main result has been the observable relationship between resource relatedness and potential synergies. Only related resources are able to enable synergy potentials. Hence, diversification seems only to be successful, if firms can build on similar resource bases. However, the astonishing finding of this survey has been the distinction of different groups of resources in R&D which are relevant for the overall generated relatedness of R&D units. Despite the arguments presented in papers following single resource concepts, the three resources 'general infrastructure', 'internal R&D knowledge' and 'operational structure' have been most relevant for the determination of relatedness of R&D units. These results have been statistically significant and are therefore able to give additional information on the consequences of resource relatedness. Hence, the concentration on single resources cannot deliver a complete picture of the interdependencies within the complex resource framework of complete functional areas. However, this book also acknowledges the weakness of these findings in terms of sample size. Therefore, a more robust empirical examination seems to be necessary to support the general applicability of the findings. Nevertheless, the descriptive results allow further detailed insights into this research area as known before.

Additionally, this book has gone further in structuring relatedness within R&D. Based on the findings of the performed survey the measurement of relatedness has been operationalised and modelled. The key intention of this more detailed assessment of relatedness was the idea to find a plain concept which is able to outline the resource relations between different R&D units. This conception concentrates on the key resources delineated above to narrow the necessary analytical work during the relatedness measurement. These information are going to be aggregated to a final figure indicating resource relatedness of R&D units. Hence, this book has build an approach to generate clear results of resource analytics and therefore is going further into the applicability of the RBV. This has been able through the introduction of a weighting concept which enables analysts to use a simple logic during the assessment of resource relatedness. This logic allows the introduction of different weightings and therefore is able to include different firm and industry specific circumstances. In a final step, the input information of this concept will be transformed into a final grade of relatedness. This result might be crucial information during the calculation of potential synergies arising through diversification. Hence, this book is not only contributing to theoretical concepts within the RBV, but also generates an approach useful during the assessment of this theoretical field in practice.

Summarised, this book has performed an extensive analysis of relatedness of R&D in the context of diversification. The theoretical background of this approach has been outlined. Based on this profound theory grounding, the actual relatedness of R&D units has been assessed. Therefore, this book has been able to give a wide range of information on this research question. Also the results of this analysis have been used to generate a measurement concept applicable for the actual measurement of relatedness of R&D units.

LIST OF REFERENCES

Abell, D. (1980): Defining the business, Englewood Cliffs, 1980.

Acs, Z.J.; Audretsch, D.B.; Feldman, M.P. (1994): R&D Spillovers and Recipient Firm Size, in: The Review of Economics and Statistics, Volume 76, Number 2, pp.336-340.

Aldenderfer, M. S.; Blashfield, R. K. (1984): Cluster analysis, Beverly Hills, 1984.

Alkhafaji, A.F. (1995): Competitive Global Management, Delray Beach, 1995.

Allen, T. J. (1977): Managing the flow of technology, Cambridge, 1977.

Amihud, Y.; Lev, B. (1981): Risk Reduction as a Managerial Motive for Conglomerate Mergers, in: Bell Journal of Economics, Volume 12, pp.605-617.

Andrews, K.R. (1951): Product diversification and the public interest, in: Harvard Business Review, Vol. 29, issue 4, pp. 91-107.

Ansoff, H.I. (1957): Strategies for diversification, in: Harvard Business Review, Vol. 35, issue 5, pp. 113-124.

Ansoff, H.I. (1965): Corporate Strategy, New York, 1965.

Anwander, A. (2000): Strategien erfolgreich verwirklichen, Berlin, 2000.

Aoshima, Y. (1993): Inter-Project Technology Transfer and the Design of Product Development Organizations, International Motor Vehicle Project, MIT Working paper.

Arora, A.; Gambardella, A. (1994): Evaluating technological information and utilizing it, in: Journal of Economic Behaviour and Organization, Vol. 24, pp. 91-114.

Audretsch, D.; Feldman, M. (1996): R&D Spillovers and the Geography of Innovation and Production, in: The American Economic Review, Vol. 86, No. 3, pp. 630-640.

Audretsch, D.; Bozeman, B.; Combs, K.; Feldman, M.; Link, A.; Siegel, D.; Stephan, P.; Tassey, G.; Wessner, C. (2002): The Economics of Science and Technology, in: Journal of Technology Transfer, Volume 27, pp.155-203.

Bainbridge, A.; Jacobsen, K.; Roos, G. (2001): Intellectual capital analysis as a strategic tool, in: Strategy and Leadership Journal, Vol. 29, Issue 4, pp. 21-26.

Bank, M.; Gerke, W. (1998): Finanzierung, Stuttgart, 1998.

Barker III, V.L.; Mueller, G.C. (2002): CEO Characteristics and Firm R&D Spending, in: Management Science, Volume 48, Number 6, pp.782-801.

Barney, J. (1991): Firm Resources and Competitive Advantage, in: Journal of Management, Volume 17, Issue 1, pp.99-120, 1991.

Barney, J. B. (1988): Returns to bidding firms in mergers and acquisitions: Reconsidering the relatedness hypothesis, in: Strategic Management Journal, Vol. 9, Special Issue, pp. 71-78.

Bartlett, C. A.; Ghoshal, S. (1998): Managing Across Borders, Bosten, 1998.

Baumol, W.J.; Panzar, J.C.; Willig, R.D. (1982): Constable Markets and the Theory of Industry Structure, New York, 1982.

Bayer AG (2004): Geschäftsbericht 2004, http://www.bayer.de/geschaeftsbericht_2004id0109/include/download/d_gb_gesamt.pdf, access date: 02.08.2006.

Becker, W.; Dietz, J. (2004): R&D cooperation and innovation activities of firms – evidence for the German manufacturing industry, in: Research Policy, Vol. 33, No. 2, pp. 209-223.

Belderbos, R.; Carree, M. A.; Diederen, B.; Lokshin, B.; Veugelers, R. (2004): Heterogeneity in R&D cooperation strategies, in: International Journal of Industrial Organization, Vol. 22, No. 7, pp. 1237-1263.

Benninghaus, H. (2001): Einführung in die sozialwissenschaftliche Datenanalyse, München, 6. Auflage.

Berger, Ph. G. and E. Ofek (1995): Diversification's Effect on Firm Value, in: Journal of Financial Economics, Volume 37, pp.39-65.

Bettis, R.A. (1981): Performance Differences in Related and Unrelated Diversified Firms, in: Strategic Management Journal, Volume 2, Issue 4, pp.379-393.

Biberacher, J. (2003): Synergiemanagement und Synergiecontrolling, München, 2003.

Bouty, I. (2000): Interpersonal and interaction influences on informal resource exchanges between R&D researchers across organizational boundaries, in: Academy of Management Journal, Vol. 43, No. 1, pp. 50-65.

Brockhoff, K. (1992): Forschung und Entwicklung, Oldenburg, 1992.

Brosius, F. (2002): SPSS 11, Bonn, 2002.

Brown, C. V.; Magill, S. L. (1998): Reconceptualizing the Context-Design Issue for the Information Systems Function, in: Organizational Science, Vol. 9, No. 2, pp. 176-194.

Brown, J. S.; Duguid, P. (1998): Organizing knowledge, in: California Management Review, Vol. 40, No. 3, pp. 90-111.

Bryman, A.; Cramer, D. (1994): Quantitative Data Analysis for Social Scientists, London, Revised Edition, 1994.

Burch, T.R.; Nada, V; Narayanan, M.P. (2000): 'Industry Structure and the Conglomerate "Discount": Theory and Evidence', Working Paper, University of Michigan.

Canals, J (2000): Managing Corporate Growth, Oxford, 2000.

Canner, N.; Mass, N. J. (2005): Turn R&D upside down, in: Research Technology Management, Vol. 48, No. 3, p. 17-21.

Capron, L.; Hulland J. (1999): Redeployment of brands, sales forces, and general marketing management expertise following horizontal acquisitions: a resource-based view, in: Journal of Marketing, Vol. 63, No. 2, pp. 41-54.

Cassiman, B.; Veugelers, R. (2002): Complementarity in the Innovation Strategy: Internal R&D, External Technology Acquisition, and Cooperation in R&D, IESE Business School Working Paper, No. 457, KU Leuven.

Caulfield, D.; Jacobson, R.; Sears, K.; Underwood, J. (2001): Fiber reinforced engineering plastics, 2nd International Conference on Advanced Wood Composites, Bethel, August 13-16, 2001.

Chandler, A. D. (1962): Strategy and Structure. Chapters in the History of the Industrial Enterprise, Cambridge, 1962.

Chatterjee, S. (1986): Type of synergy and economic value: The impact of acquisitions on merging and rival firms, in: Strategic Management Journal, Volume 7, Issue 2, pp.119-139.

Chatterjee, S.; Wernerfelt, B. (1991): The link between resources and type of diversification: theory and evidence, in: Strategic Management Journal, Vol. 12, No. 1, pp. 33-48.

Chen, T.-Y. (2002): Measuring firm performance with DEA an prior information in Taiwan's banks, in: Applied Economics Letters, Volume 9, pp.201-204.

Chiang, C.C.; Mensah, Y.M. (2004): The Determinants of Investor Valuation of R&D Expenditure in the Software Industry, in: Review of Quantitative Finance and Accounting, Volume 22, pp.293-313.

Coase, R.H. (1937); 'The nature of the firm', Economica, New Series IV, pp. 386-405.

Coccia, M. (2004): New models for measuring the R&D performance and identifying the productivity of public research institutes, in: R&D Management, Vol. 34, No. 3, pp. 267-280.

Cohen, W.; Klepper, S. (1996): Firm Size and the Nature of Innovation Within Industries: The Case of Process and Product R&D, in: Review of Economics and Statistics, Vol. 78, No. 2, pp. 232-243.

Cohen, W.; Levin, R. (1989): Empirical studies of innovation and market structure, in: Schmalensee, R.; Willig, R. (Eds.), Handbook of Industrial Organisation II, Amsterdam, pp. 1060-1107.

Collis, D. J.; Montgomery, C. A. (1998): Creating Corporate Advantage, in: Harvard Business Review, Vol. 76, No. 3, pp. 70-83.

Damanpour, F. (1992): Organizational size and innovation, in: Organization Studies, Vol. 13, No. 3, pp. 375-402.

Davis, R.; Duhaime, I.M. (1992): Diversification, Vertical Integration, and Industry Analysis: New Perspectives and Measurement, in: Strategic Management Journal, Volume 13, Number 7, pp.511-524.

Davis, R.; Thomas, L. G. (1993): Direct estimation of synergy: a new approach to the diversity performance debate, in: Management Science, Vol. 39, No. 11, pp. 1334-1346.

Day, G. (1981): The Product Life Cycle: Analysis and Application Issues, in: Journal of Marketing, Vol. 45, No. 4, pp. 60-67.

Del Canto, J. G.; Gonzalez, I. S. (1999): A resource-based analysis of the factors determining a firm's R&D activities, in: Research Policy, Vol. 28, No. 8, pp. 891-905.

Diekmann, A. (2004): Empirische Sozialforschung – Grundlagen, Methoden, Anwendungen -, 12. Auflage, Reinbek bei Hamburg, 2004.

Dierickx, I.; Cool, K. (1989): Asset Stock Accumulation and Sustainability of Competitive Advantage, in: Management Science, Volume 35, Issue 12, pp.1504-1511.

Döhmen, H.P. (1991): Anlässe, Ziele und Methodik der Diversifikation. Dargestellt am Beispiel einer Unternehmung der Asphaltindustrie, Bergisch-Gladbach/Köln, 1991.

DTI (Department of Trade and Industry) (2005): The 2005 R&D Scoreboard – The top 750 UK and 1000 Global companies by R&D investment- Commentary and Analysis Volume 1, http://www.innovation.gov.uk/rd_scoreboard/downloads/RD_Analysis_20051%20-%20FINAL.pdf, access date: 12.06.2006.

Edler, J. (2001): The Management of Knowledge in German Industry, http://www.segera.ruc.dk/Jacob%20Edler.pdf, access date: 11.07.2006.

Edvinsson, L. (1997): Developing intellectual capital at Skandia, in: Long Range Planning, Vol. 30, No. 3, pp. 320-331.

Ensign, P.C. (2004): A Resource-based View of Interrelationships among Organizational Groups in the Diversified Firm, in: Strategic Change, Volume 13, Issue 3, p.125-137.

Evangelista, R.; Sandven, T.; Sirilli, G.; Smith, K. (1998): Measuring Innovation in European Industry, in: International Journal of the Economics of Business, Vol. 5, No. 3, pp. 311-333.

Farjoun, M. (1994): Beyond Industry Boundaries: Human Expertise, Diversification and Resource-related Industry Groups, in: Organization Science, Vol. 5, No. 2, pp. 185-199.

Farjoun, M. (1998): The independent and joint effects of the skill and physical bases of relatedness in diversification, in: Strategic Management Journal, Vol. 19, No. 7, pp. 611-630.

Fey, A. (1999): Diversifikation und Unternehmensstrategie – Zur Insuffizienz der Analyse des Diversifikationserfolges in der empirischen Diversifikationsforschung, Dissertation, Fernuniversität Hagen, Frankfurt am Main, 1999.

Fischer, M.; Fröhlich, J.; Gassler, H. (1994): An Exploration into the Determinants of Patent Activities: Some Empirical Evidence for Austria, in: Regional Studies, Volume 28, pp.1-12.

Fleming, L. (2001): Recombinant uncertainty in technological search, in: Management Science, Vol. 47, No. 1, pp. 117-132.

Forte, M. (2002): Unschärfen in Geschäftsprozessen, Dissertation, Berlin, 2002.

Foss, N.J. (1998): The Resource-Based Perspective: An Assessment and Diagnosis of Problems, in: Scandinavian Journal of Management, Volume 14, Issue 3, pp.133-149.

Fritsch, M.; Lukas, R. (2001): Who cooperates on R&D?, in: Research Policy, Vol. 30, No. 2, pp. 297-312.

Frommann, L.K. (2002): Quantitative Erfolgsfaktoren bei der Vorbereitung von Bankenfusionen unter besonderer Berücksichtigung der Bankenbewertung, Dissertation, Bern, 2002.

Fry, T.; Jarvis, K.; Loundes, J. (2002): Are Pro-Performers Better Performers?, in: Melbourne Institute Working Paper, Number 18/02, http://www.melbourneinstitute.com/wp/wp2002n18.pdf, access date: 03.08.2006.

Galunic, D.Ch.; Rodan, S. (1998): Resource recombinations in the firm: knowledge structures and the potential for Schumpeterian innovation, in: Strategic Management Journal, Vol. 25, Issue 6, pp. 1193-1201.

Ganz, M. (1991): Die Erhöhung des Unternehmenswertes durch die Strategie der externen Diversifikation, Dissertation, Hochschule St. Gallen, Bern, 1991.

Garcia-Valderrama, T.; Mulero-Mendigorri, E. (2005): Content validation of a measure of R&D effectiveness, in: R&D Management, Vol. 35, No. 3, pp. 311-331.

Gassenheimer, J.B.; Keep, W.W. (1998): 'Generalizing diversification theory across economic sectors: theoretical and empirical considerations', in Journal of Marketing Theory and Practice, Vol. 6, Issue 1, pp. 38-47.

Gassmann, O. (1997): Organisationsformen der internationalen F&E in technologie-intensiven Grossunternehmen, in: Zeitschrift Führung und Organisation, Vol. 66, No. 6, pp. 332-339.

Gassmann, O.; von Zedtwitz, M. (1998): Organization of industrial R&D on a global scale, in: R&D Management, Vol. 28, No. 3, pp. 147-161.

Gassmann, O.; von Zedtwitz, M. (1999): New concepts and trends in international R&D organization, in: Research Policy, Vol. 28, pp. 231-250.

Gassmann, O.; Han, Z. (2004): Motivations and barriers of foreign R&D activities in China, in: R&D Management, Vol. 34, No. 4, pp. 423-437.

Gebert, F. (1983): Diversifikation und Organisation. Die organisatorische Eingliederung von Diversifikation , Frankfurt am Main u.a., 1983.

Gerke, W.; Bank, M. (2003): Finanzierung -Grundlagen für Investitions- und Finanzierungsentscheidungen in Unternehmen-, 2.überarbeitete und erweiterte Auflage, Stuttgart, 2003.

Gerybadze, A.; Meyer-Krahmer, F.; Reger, G.: Globales Management von Forschung und Innovation, Stuttgart, 1997.

Gilsing, V.; Erken, H. (2002): Trends in corporate R&D, Ministry of Economic Affairs working paper, The Hague, 2002.

Goold, M. and A. Campbell (1998): Desperately Seeking Synergy, in: Harvard Business Review, Volume 76, issue 5, pp. 131-146, 1998.

Gort, M. (1962): Diversification and integration in American industry, Princeton, 1962.

Grant, R. M. (1988): On 'Dominant Logic', Relatedness and the Link between Diversity and Performance, in: Strategic Management Journal, Vol. 9, Issue 8, pp. 639-642.

Grimm, A. (1986): Motive konglomerater Unternehmenszusammenschlüsse: Analyse der theoretischen Erklärungsansätze und Fallstudien grosser

Zusammenschlüsse in den USA, Dissertation, Universität Hamburg, Göttingen, 1986.

Grindley, P.C.; Teece, D.J. (1997): Managing Intellectual Capital: Licensing and Cross-Licensing in Semiconductors and Electronics, in: California Management Review, Volume 39, Number 2, pp.8-41.

Hall, R. (1992): The strategic analysis of intangible resources, in Strategic Management Journal, Vol. 13, No. 2, pp. 135-144.

Hargadon, A. B. (1998): Firms as knowledge brokers. Lessons in pursuing continuous innovation, in: California Management Review, Vol. 40, No. 3, pp. 209-227.

Harhoff, D. (1998): Are there Financing Constraints for R&D investment in German Manufacturing Firms?, in: Annales d'Economie et de Statistique, Number 49/50, pp.421-456.

Harrison, J. S.; Hall, E. H.; Nargundkar, R. (1993): Resource allocation as an outcropping of strategic consistency: performance implications, in: Academy of Management Journal, Vol. 36, No. 5, pp. 1026-1051.

Harrison, J. S.; Hitt, M. A.; Hoskisson, R. E.; Ireland, R. D. (2001): Resource complementarity in business combinations: Extending the logic to organizational alliances, in: Journal of Management, Vol. 27, No. 6, pp. 679-690.

Heilmann, M. (1996): Geschäftsprozess-Controlling, Dissertation, Bern, 1996.

Henderson, R.; Cockburn, I. (1994): Measuring competence? Exploring firm effects in pharmaceutical research, in: Strategic Management Journal, Vol. 16, No. 1, pp. 63-84.

HGB (2006): www.handelsgesetzbuch.de, access date: 10.08.2006.

Hill, C.W.L.; Hitt, M.A.; Hoskisson, R.E. (1992): "Cooperative versus Competitive Structures in Related and Unrelated Diversified Firms", in: Organization Science, Vol. 3 Issue 4, pp.501-521.

Hirst, G.; Mann, L. (2004): A model of R&D leadership and team communication: the relationship with project performance, in: R&D Management, Vol. 34, No. 2, pp. 147-160.

Hitt, M. A.; Hoskisson, R. E.; Ireland, R. D.; Harrison, J. S. (1991): Effects of Acquisitions on R&D Inputs and Outputs, in: Academy of Management Journal, Vol. 34, No. 3, pp. 693-706.

Hoskisson, R.E.; Hitt, M.A.; Johnson, R.A.; Moesel, D.D. (1993): "Construct Validity of an Objective (Entropy) Categorial Measure of Diversification Strategy, in: Strategic Management Journal, Volume 14, Number 3, pp.215-235.

Hoskisson, R.E.; Hitt, M.A.; Wan, W.P.; Yiu, D. (1999): Theory and research in strategic management: Swings of a pendulum, in: Journal of Management, Volume 25, Issue 3, pp.417-456.

Hungenberg, H. (2001): Strategisches Management in Unternehmen: Ziele – Prozesse – Verfahren, 2. Auflage, Wiesbaden, 2001.

Hungenberg, H. (2002): Problemlösung und Kommunikation, 2. Auflage, Oldenburg, 2002.

Hübler, O. (2005): Einführung in die empirische Sozialforschung –Probleme, Methoden und Anwendungen-, München, 2005.

Ilinitch, A.Y.; Zeithaml, C.P. (1995): Operationalizing and Testing Galbraith's Center of Gravity Theory, in: Strategic Management Journal, Volume 16, pp.401-410.

Itami, H. (1987): Mobilizing Invisible Assets, Cambridge, 1987.

Jacobson, R. (1992): The "Austrian" School of Strategy, in: The Academy of Management Review, Vol. 17, No. 4, pp. 782-807.

Jankowski, J. (2001): Measurement and Growth of R&D Within the Service Economy, in: Journal of Technology Transfer, Vol. 26, pp. 323-336.

Jensen, M.C.; Meckling W. H. (1976): Theory of the Firm: Managerial Behavior, Agency Costs, and Ownership Structure, in: Journal of Financial Economics, Volume 3, pp.305-360.

Jones, G. R.; Hill, C. W. L. (1988): Transaction Cost Analysis of Strategy-Structure Choice, in: Strategic Management Journal, Vol. 9, No. **, pp. 159-172.

Jose, M.L.; Nichols, L.M.; Stevens, J.L. (1986): Contributions of diversification, promotion, and R&D to the value of multiproduct firms: A Tobin`s q approach, in: Financial Management, Volume 15, pp.33-42.

Josephson, M. (1959): Edison: A Biography, New York, 1959.

Katz, R.; Allen, T. J. (1988): Investigating the not invented here (NIH) syndrome, in: Tushman, M. L.; Moore, W. L. (eds.), Readings in the Management of Innovation, 2nd edition, Cambridge, 1988, pp. 293-301.

Kanter, R. M. (1998): Seeking and Achieving Synergies, in: A. Campbell and K. Luchs (eds.): Strategic Synergy (2nd edition), London: International Thomson Business Press, 1998.

Khurana, A. (2006): Strategies for Global R&D, in: Research Technology Management, Vol. 49, No. 2, pp. 48-57.

Kim, K; Park, J-H.; Prescott, J. (2003): The global integration of business functions: a study of multinational businesses in integrated global industries, in: Journal of International Business Studies, Vol. 34, No. 4, pp. 327-344.

Klein, I.; Missong, M. (2002): Deskriptive Statistik, Kiel und Nürnberg, 2002.

Klepper, S. (1996): Entry, Exit, Growth, and Innovation over the Product Life Cycle, in: American Economic Review, Vol. 86, No. 3, pp. 562-583.

Kohli, R.; Devaraj, S (2003): Measuring Information Technology Payoff: A Meta-Analysis of Structural Variables in Firm-Level Empirical Research, in: Information Systems Research, Volume 14, No. 2, pp.127-145.

Koruna, S. (2004): Leveraging knowledge assets: combinative capabilities – theory and practice, in: R&D Management, Vol. 34, No. 5, pp. 505-516.

Kostopoulos, K. C.; Spanos, Y. E.; Prastacos, G. P. (2002): The Resource-Based View of the Firm and Innovation: Identification of Critical Linkages, EURAM Second Annual Conference, Innovative Research in Management, Stockholm.

Kothari, S.; Languerre, T.; Leone, A. (2002): Capitalization versus Expensing: Evidence on the Uncertainty of Future Earnings from Capital Expenditures versus R&D Outlays, in: Review of Accounting Studies, Vol. 4, No. 4, pp. 355-382.

Kuemmerle, W. (1998): Optimal scale for research and development in foreign environments – an investigation into size and performance of research and development laboratories abroad, in: Research Policy, Vol. 27, No. 2, pp. 111-126.

Lam, A. (2003): Organizational Learning in Multinationals: R&D Networks of Japanese and US MNEs in the UK, in: Journal of Management Studies, Vol. 40, No. 3, pp. 673-703.

Lehmann, R. (1993): Kann Diversifikation Wert schaffen?, Stuttgart, 1993.

Leitner, K.-H. (2005): Managing and reporting intangible assets in research technology organisations, in: R&D Management, Vol. 35, No. 2, pp. 125-136.

Lemelin, A. (1982): Relatedness in the Patterns of Interindustry Diversification, in: Review of Economics and Statistics, Volume 64, pp.646-657.

Leonard-Barton, D (1992): Core capabilities and core rigidities: a paradox in managing new product development, in: Strategic Management Journal, Vol. 13, Summer Special Issue, pp. 111-125.

Lewellen, W.G. (1971): A Pure Financial Rationale for Conglomerate Merger, in: Journal of Finance, Volume 26, pp.521-537.

Lieberman, M.B.; Montgomery, D.B. (1998): First-Mover (Dis)Advantages: Retrospective and Link with the Resource-Based View, in: Strategic Management Journal, Volume 19, pp.1111-1125.

Limmack, R.J.; McGregor, N. (1995): Industrial relatedness, structural factors and bidder returns, in: Applied Financial Economics, Volume 5, p.179-190, 1995.

Löbler, H. (1988): Diversifikation und Unternehmenserfolg: Diversifikationserfolge und –risiken bei unterschiedlichen Marktstrukturen und Wettbewerb, Wiesbaden, 1988.

Long, W.; Ravenscraft, D. (1993): LBOs, debt and R&D intensity, in: Strategic Management Journal, Vol. 14, Summer Special Issue, pp. 119-135.

Lundholm, R.; O'Keefe T. (2001): Reconciling Value Estimates from the Discounted Cash Flow Model and the Residual Income Model, in: Contemporary Accounting Research, Vol. 18, No. 2, pp. 311-335.

Lynskey, M. J. (1999): The Transfer of Resources and Competencies for Developing Technological Capabilities – The Case of Fujitsu-ICL, in: Technology Analysis & Strategic Management, Vol. 11, No. 3, pp. 317-336.

Markides, C.C.; Williamson, P.J. (1994): Related Diversification, Core Competences and Corporate Performance, in: Strategic Management Journal, Volume 15, pp.149-165, 1994.

Markides, C. C.; Williamson, P. J. (1996): Corporate Diversification and Organizational Structure: A Resource-Based View, in: Academy of Management Journal, Vol. 39, No. 2, pp. 340-367.

Marshall, W.J.; Yawitz J. B.; Greenberg E. (1984): Incentives for Diversification and the Structure of the Conglomerate Firm, in: Southern Economic Journal, Volume 51, pp.1-23.

Mason, E. (1939): Price and Production Policies of Large-Scale Enterprise, in: American Economic Review, Volume 29, Issue 1, pp. 61-74.

Michel, A.; Shaked, I. (1984): Does business diversification affect performance?, in: Financial Management, Volume 13, Issue 4, pp.18-25.

Miles, M.B.; Huberman, A.M. (1994): -An Expanded Sourcebook- Qualitative Data Analysis, Second Edition, Thousand Oaks, 1994.

Milgrom, P.; Roberts, J. (1995): Complementarities and fit strategy, structure, and organizational change in manufacturing, in: Journal of Accounting and Economics, Vol. 19, No. 2-3, pp. 179-208.

Miller, D.J. (2006): Technological Diversity, Related Diversification, and Firm Performance, in: Strategic Management Journal, Volume 27, pp.601-619.

Minderlein, M. (1993): Industrieökonomik und Strategieforschung, in: Staehle/Sydow (1993), Managementforschung 3, Berlin, pp.157-201, 1993.

Montgomery, C.A. (1985): Product-Market Diversification and Market Power, in: Academy of Management Journal, Volume 28, pp.789-798.

Montgomery, C.A. (1994): Corporate Diversification, in: Journal of Economic Perspectives, Vol. 8, No. 3, 1994, pp. 163-178.

Montgomery, C.A.; Hariharan, S. (1991): Diversified expansion by large established firms, in: Journal of Economics, Behaviour and Organization, Volume 15, pp.71-89.

Narula, R. (2003): Globalisation and trends in international R&D alliances, in: MERIT-Infonomics Research Memorandum series, Vol. 2003, No. 1, 2003.

Narula, R.; Duysters, G. (2004): Globalization and Trends in International R&D Alliances, in: Journal of International Management, Vol. 10, p. 199-218.

National Science Foundation (2006): Basic Research, Applied Research and Development (B, A, D) by Industry and Source [1953-98], http://www.nsf.go/ statistics/iris/search_hist.cfm?indx=9, accessed 27.04.2006.

Nayak, P. R.; Ketteringham, J. M. (1986): Breakthroughs!, New York, 1986.

Nayyar, P. (1992): The Measurement of Corporate Diversification Strategy: Evidence from Large U.S. Service Firms, in: Strategic Management Journal, 1992, pp.219-235.

Novartis (2006): NIBR — Current alliances, http://www.nibr.novartis.com/ StrategicAlliances/current_alliances.shtml, access date, 22.05.2006.

O'Dell, C.; Grayson, C. J. (1998): If Only We Knew What We Know, New York, 1998.

OECD (1992): Technology and the Economy, Paris, 1992.

OECD (1998): Co-operative Behaviour of Innovative Firms in Austria, Paris, 1998.

OECD (2002): Frascati Manual 2002, Paris, 2002

Osiris (2006): Datenbanksystem, issued by Bureau van DIJK, http://www.bvdep.com/OSIRIS.html, access date: 10.04.2006.

Palepu, K.G. (1985): Diversification strategy, profit performance, and the entropy measure, in: Strategic Management Journal, Volume 6, Issue 3, pp.239-255, 1985.

Palich, L. E.; Cardinal, L. B.; Miller, C. C. (2000): Curvilinearity in the Diversification-Performance Linkage. An Examination of Three Decades of Research, in: Strategic Management Journal, Vol. 6, pp. 239-255.

Patel, P.; Pavit, K. (1991): Large firms in the production of the world's technology: an important case of 'non-globalisation', in: Journal of International Business Stuedies, Vol. 22. No. 1, pp. 1-21.

Pearson, G. J. (1989): Promoting entrepreneurship in large companies, in: Long Range Planning, Vol. 22, No. 3, pp. 87-97.

Peemöller, V.H. (2003): Bilanzanalyse und Bilanzpolitik, Wiesbaden, 3. Auflage, 2003.

Penrose, E. (1963): The theory of the growth of the firm, Oxford, 1963.

Peteraf, M.A. (1993): The Cornerstones of Competitive Advantage. A Resource-based View, in: Strategic Management Journal, Volume 14, pp.179-191,1993.

Pfeffer, J.; Sutton, R. I. (2000): The Knowing-Doing Gap: How Smart Companies Turn Knowledge into Action, Boston, 2000.

Pike, S.; Roos, G.; Marr, B. (2005): Strategic management of intangible assets and value drivers in R&D organizations, in: R&D Management, Vol. 35, No. 2, pp. 111-124.

Porter, M.E. (1985): Competitive Advantage, New York, 1985.

Porter, M. E. (1987): From Competitive Advantage to Corporate Strategy, in: Harvard Business Review, May/June, pp. 43-59.

Porter, M. E. (1990): The competitive advantage of nations, New York, 1990.

Prahalad, C.K.; Bettis, R.A. (1986): The Dominant Logic: A New Linkage between Diversity and Performance, in: Strategic Management Journal, Volume 7, Issue 6, pp.485-501.

Prahalad, C. K.; Bettis, R. A. (1995): The Dominant Logic: Retrospective and Extension, in: Strategic Management Journal, Vol. 16, No. 1, pp. 5-14.

Prahalad, C. K.; Hamel, G. (1990): The Core Competence of the Corporation, in: Harvard Business Review, Vol. 68, No. 3, pp. 79-91.

Quelin, B. (2000): Core competencies, R&D management and partnerships, in: European Management Journal, Vol. 18, No. 5, pp. 476-487.

Quinn, J. B. (1985): Managing Innovation: Controlled Chaos, in: Harvard Business Review, Vol. 63, No. 3, pp. 73-84.

Ramanujam, V.; Varadarajan, P. (1989): Research on corporate diversification, in: Strategic Management Journal, Volume 10, pp.523-551.

Reed, R.; Luffman, G. A. (1986): Diversification: The Growing Confusion, in: Strategic Management Journal, Volume 7, pp.29-35.

Robins, J. A.; Wiersema, M. F. (1995): A resource-based approach to the multi-business firm: empirical analysis of portfolio interrelationships and corporate financial performance, in: Strategic Management Journal, Vol. 16, No. 4, pp. 277-299.

Rogers, M. (2002): Firm Performance and Investment in R&D and Intellectual Property, in: Melbourne Institute Working Paper, Number 15/02, http://melbourneinstitute.com/wp/wp2002n15.pdf, access date: 02.08.2006.

Rogers, D. (1996): The Challenge of Fifth Generation R&D, in: Research Technology Management, Vol. 39, No. 4, pp. 33-41.

Rosenberg, N. (1994): Exploring the black box, Cambridge, 1994.

Roussel, P.; Saad, K.; Erickson, T.: Third Gereration R&D: Managing the Link to Corporate Strategy, Boston, 1991.

Rühli, E.; Sachs, S. (2000): Die zentralen Kernkompetenzen der diversifizierten Unternehmung, in: Die Zukunft der diversifizierten Unternehmung, Editor: Hinterhuber, H.H.; Friedrich, S.A.; Matzler, K.; Pechlaner, H., München, p.127-145, 2000.

Rumelt, R. (1982): Diversification strategy and profitability, in: Strategic Management Journal, Volume 3, pp. 359-369.

Rumelt, R. (1984): Towards a strategic theory of the firm, in: Lamb (Ed.), Competitive strategic management, Englewood Cliffs, pp. 556-570, 1984.

Rummelt, R.; Schendel, D.; Teece, D. J. (1991): Strategic Management and Economics, in: Strategic Management Journal, Vol. 12, Winter Special Issue, pp. 5-29.

Sauer, I.; Alves, J.; Marques, M. J. (2005): R&D in multidisciplinary and cross-organizational environments: multisectoral networks for innovation, Paper to be presented at The R&D Management Conference 2005, Italy, 2005.

Scharfstein, D.; J. Stein (2000): "The dark side of internal capital markets: Divisional rentseeking and inefficient investment", The Journal of Finance, Vol. 55, Issue 6, pp. 2537-2564.

Scherer, F.M. (1982): Intra-industry technology flows in the US, in: Research Policy, Volume 11, pp.227-245.

Schmidt, S.L.; Vogt, P.; Schriber, S. (2005): Ansätze und Ergebnisse anglo-amerikanischer M&A-Forschung, in: Journal für Betriebswirtschaft, Volume 55, Number 4, pp.297-319.

Schnell, R.; Hill, P.B.; Esser, E. (1993): Methoden der empirischen Sozialforschung, München, 4. überarbeitete Auflage, 1993.

Schulze, W.S. (1994): The two schools of thought in resource-based theory: Definitions and implications for research, in: Advances in Strategic Management, Volume 10A, pp.127-154.

Schumpeter, J. (1943): Capitalism, Socialism and Democracy, second edition, London, 1943.

Scott, J. H., Jr. (1977): On the Theory of Conglomerate Mergers, in: Journal of Finance, Volume 32, pp.1235-1250.

Siegel, D. (1997): The impact of computers on manufacturing productivity growth: Multiple-Indicators, Multiple-Causes Approach, in: Review of Economics and Statistics, Volume 79, Issue 1, pp.68-78.

Silverman, B. S. (1999): Technological Resources and the Direction of Corporate Diversification: Toward an Integration of the Resource-Based View and Transaction Cost Economics, in: Management Science, Vol. 45, No. 8, pp. 1109-1124.

Sogaard, V. (2001): Bayer AG – Chemicals And Life Sciences, in: AgBioForum, Vol. 4, No. 1, pp. 68-73.

Solow, R. (1957): Technical change and the aggregate production function, in: Review of Economics and Statistics, Vol. 39, pp. 312-320.

Song, M.; Droge, C.; Hanavanich, S.; Calantone, R. (2005): Marketing and technology resource complementarity: an analysis of their interaction effect in two environmental contexts, in: Strategic Management Journal, Vol. 26, No. 3, pp. 259-276.

Souitaris, V. (2002): Firm-specific competencies determining technological innovations: a survey in Greece, in: R&D Management, Vol. 32, No. 1, pp. 61-77.

St. John, C.H. and J.S. Harrison (1999): Manufacturing-based Relatedness, Synergy, and Coordination, in: Strategic Management Journal, Volume 20, pp.129-145, 1999.

Steinemann, P. P. (1999): R&D Strategies for New Automotive Technologies: Insights from Fuel Cells, MIT Working Paper, International Motor Vehicle Program (IMVP), http://imvp.mit.edu/papers/99/fuelcell.pdf, access date 16.06.2006.

Stier, W. (1999): Empirische Forschungsmethoden, 2. Auflage, Berlin, 1999.

Stimpert, J.L.; Duhaime, I.M. (1997): In the Eyes of the Beholder: Conceptualizations of Relatedness held by the Managers of large diversified Firms, in: Strategic Management Journal, Volume 18, Issue 2, pp.111-125.

Stulz, R. M. (1990): Managerial Discretion and Optimal Financing Policies, in: Journal of Financial Economics, Volume 26, pp.3-27.

Szeless, G.; Wiersema, M.F.; Müller-Stewens, G. (2000): Relatedness and Firm Performance in European Firms: A Comparison of Related Entropy and Resource-Based Relatedness, IfB Diskussionsbeiträge, Universität St. Gallen.

Szeless, G. (2001): Diversifikation und Unternehmenserfolg, Dissertation der Universität St. Gallen, St. Gallen, 2001.

Tanriverdi, H. (2005): Information Technology Relatedness, Knowledge Management Capability, and Performance of Multi-business Firms, in: MIS Quarterly, Vol. 29, No. 2, pp. 311-334.

Tanriverdi, H. (2006): Performance Effects of Information Technology Synergies in Multi-business Firms, in: MIS Quaterly, Vol. 30, No. 1, pp. 57-77.

Tanriverdi, H.; Venkatraman, N. (2004): Knowledge Relatedness and the Performance of Multi-business Firms, in Strategic Management Journal, Volume 26, pp. 97-119.

Taylor, W. (1990): The Business of Innovation: An Interview with Paul Cook, in: Harvard Business Review, March/April, pp. 97-106.

Teece, D. J. (1980): Economics of scope and the scope of the enterprise, in: Journal of Economic Behavior and Organization, Vol. 1, No. 3, pp. 223-247.

Teece, D. J. (1982): Towards an Economic Theory of the Multiproduct Firm, in: Journal of Economic Behavior and Organization, Vol. 3, Issue 1, pp. 39-63.

Teece, D. J. (1986): Profiting from technological innovation: Implications for integration, collaboration, licensing and public policy, in: Research Policy, Vol. 15, Issue 6, pp. 285-305.

Tolpert, A. S.; McLean, G. N.; Myers, R. C. (2002): Creating the global learning organization (GLO), in: International Journal of Intercultural Relations, Vol. 26, No. 4, pp. 463-472.

Varadarajan, P. (1986): Product diversity and firm performance: An empirical investigation, in: Journal of Marketing, Volume 59, Issue 3, pp.43-57.

Varadarajan, P.; Ramanujam, V. (1987): Diversification and performance: A re-examination using a new two-dimensional conceptualization of diversity in firms, in: Academy of Management Journal, Volume 30, pp.380-397.

Veugelers, R. (1998): Collaboration in R&D: An assessment of theoretical and empirical findings, in: De Economist, Vol. 146, No. 3, pp. 419-443.

Villalonga, B. (2004): Diversification Discount or Premium? New Evidence from the Business Information Tracking Series, in: The Journal of Finance, Volume 59, Issue 2, pp.479-506.

Volberda, H. W. (1998): Building the Flexible Firm: How to Remain Competitive, Oxford, 1998.

Wade, M.; Hulland, J. (2004): Review: The Resource-Based View and Information Systems Research: Review, Extension, and Suggestions for Future Research, in: MIS Quarterly, Vol. 28, No. 1, pp. 107-142.

Wernerfelt, B. (1984): A Resource-based View of the Firm, in: Strategic Management Journal, Volume 5, pp.171-180.

Wolff, M. F. (1996): Perspectives, in: Research Technology Management, Vol. 39, No. 5, pp. 2-8.

Yeoh, P-L.; Roth, K. (1999): An empirical analysis of sustained advantage in the U.S. pharmaceutical industry: impact of firm resources and capabilities, in: Strategic Management Journal, Vol. 20, No. 7, pp. 637-653.

VDM

Verlag
Dr. Müller

Wissenschaftlicher Buchverlag bietet

kostenfreie

Publikation

von aktuellen

wissenschaftlichen Arbeiten

Diplomarbeiten, Magisterarbeiten, Master und Bachelor Theses
sowie Dissertationen und wissenschaftliche Monographien

innerhalb von Fachbuchprojekten
(Monographien und Sammelwerke)

**in den Fachgebieten Wirtschafts- und Sozialwissenschaften
sowie Wirtschaftsinformatik.**

Sie verfügen über eine Arbeit zu aktuellen Fragestellungen aus den genannten
Fachgebieten, die hohen inhaltlichen und formalen Ansprüchen genügt,
und haben **Interesse an einer honorarvergüteten Publikation**?

Dann senden Sie bitte erste Informationen über sich und Ihre Arbeit per Email
an info@vdm-verlag.de. Unser Außenlektorat meldet sich umgehend bei Ihnen.

VDM Verlag Dr. Mueller e.K. · Dudweiler Landstraße 125a
D - 66123 Saarbrücken · www.vdm-buchverlag.de

Printed in the United Kingdom
by Lightning Source UK Ltd.
132337UK00001B/5/A